creative ESSENTIALS

KAROL GRIFFITHS

THE ART OF SCRIPT EDITING
A PRACTICAL GUIDE

creative ESSENTIALS

First published in 2015 by Kamera Books
an imprint of Oldcastle Books,
PO Box 394, Harpenden, Herts, AL5 1XJ
www.kamerabooks.com

ISBN
978-1-84344-507-4 (print)
978-1-84344-508-1 (epub)
978-1-84344-509-8 (kindle)
978-1-84344-510-4 (pdf)

2 4 6 8 10 9 7 5 3 1
Typeset by Elsa Mathern in Franklin Gothic 9 pt
Printed by CPI Group (UK) ltd, Croydon, CR0 4YY

In loving memory of my mother and father

ACKNOWLEDGEMENTS

In preparing this book, I sought out the support and expertise of some very talented and accomplished industry professionals; I am extremely grateful to Hossein Amini, Paul Mayhew-Archer, John August, Hayley McKenzie, Robyn Slovo, Ludo Smolski and Paul Matthew Thompson for generously sharing their treasured insights and valuable time, and helping me to investigate the joys and challenges of script editing and story development.

Additional thanks to...

Rebecca Swift for her kind support, guidance and friendship.

Lucy Scher for her valuable instruction during my transition to the United Kingdom.

Sven Angelbauer, Lisa Barr, Kathy Bell, Tarryn Campbell-Gillies, Martin Casella, Darin Elliott, Jean Kaye, Michael Sierton and Nancy Smalling for being such wonderful friends – and giving me the support and confidence to get through this crazy year.

My profound thanks go to Hannah Patterson and Ion Mills for inviting me to write this book, and for supporting me along the way; and to the dedicated team at Kamera Books, who have been fantastic: Claire Watts, Anne Hudson, Elsa Mathern, Jayne Lewis and Steven Mair.

Love and gratitude to my family: Pamela Merrick, Laurel Goldman, the Viriet family, the Siegel clan, Sue Gurley, Jane Goldberg, Lucy and Ollie, and ESPECIALLY to John – you are the most amazing husband in the world – thanks for being mine.

CONTENTS

INTRODUCTION

A CAREER IN SCRIPT DEVELOPMENT

Working in script development is a mercurial existence to say the least – a roller coaster ride with endless twists and turns. The highs are exciting, engaging and gratifying and the lows are equally potent, often filled with disappointment, sleepless nights and utter frustration. BUT when the process succeeds, it is undoubtedly one of the most satisfying and privileged roles in the entertainment industry.

The aim of this book is to demystify the process: to offer insight into how to find, nurture and foster screenwriters, to explain how script editors and development teams work with writers, producers and executives within the system, and to give writers an understanding of how they can most effectively work with a script editor and within a development team.

For writers, the development process can quickly become a confusing labyrinth. It might not seem like it, but screenwriting is a collaborative job, and although writers spend much of their time working alone, writing for film and television is ultimately all about working with others. The initial idea and first draft are just the beginning, because from that point onwards, everyone will have an opinion on how to develop the story. From inception up until the final polish, even into post-production and every step along the way, there will be outside input, comments, ideas and conflicting notes to navigate through. Just about everyone involved in the process will have an opinion or an agenda – even well-meaning friends and family will eagerly offer up comments. So, it's no wonder that writers frequently become overwhelmed.

THE ART OF SCRIPT EDITING

Filmmaking is an expensive and pressured business and decision makers need to be secure in the projects and scripts that they are responsible for selecting. So, it's understandable that everyone has an opinion, because there is a lot at stake. From the entry-level readers on up until the executive producer – it's their reputations, careers and possibly even money on the line. Even a low-budget, indie film is costly, time-consuming and takes a great deal of hard work to produce – so everyone wants to get it right.

Readers and development teams are inundated with piles of scripts. Their job is to filter out the unworthy, and to find a precious diamond in the rough. They worry constantly, desperate not to reject what might be a successful blockbuster and equally concerned about putting through a disappointing and expensive failure.

Agents are concerned with getting their writers work, but also with earning commissions. They often use their hard-earned insider information to influence writers into reworking ideas to fit a trend or brief – hoping to provide the type of script that producers say they are looking for.

At the producer level, there are other concerns: practicality, financial ramifications and market requirements. Again, these often lead to more notes for the writer. Studio executives and commissioners will have even more thoughts, such as attaching talent, and needing a balanced slate of projects. Maybe they only produce one drama feature a year, but are willing to consider a script if it's tailored for specific talent they have a relationship with. The lead character may have been written as a 20-something ingénue, but the actor they have in mind is middle-aged – and so, the writer will once again have to consider making changes and possibly implement extensive revisions in the hopes of getting the film made.

Even when the script gets a green light and makes it into production, the development and collaboration doesn't end. Elements continually evolve, constantly shift and change. At that juncture, creative talent has influence and yet more questions, concerns and rewrites need to be addressed – and are sometimes demanded.

Consequently, it can be a long and difficult journey getting a script ready for production and hard for a writer to know which direction to take while also trying to maintain the integrity of their vision along the way.

So what is a script editor's role during all this?

I am asked this question regularly, and often even by people who work in the industry. The answer is quite simple, although the job is far from it.

The role of a script editor is to help the writer successfully tell their story in a way that connects with their intended audience.

Script editors are usually highly educated graduates, with extensive experience as script readers, and proven analytical skills in the art of storytelling. They work extremely closely with the writer and must have a comprehensive knowledge of the screenwriting theories used by writers and producers to guide their work. They are there to help the writer get through the development maze and to support the writing.

A script editor will examine the script and provide an analytical overview of the work. They will identify any problem areas and assess where the script is working and where and why it is not; and they aim to help the writer get on, stay on track.

A good script editor will simplify the process, helping the writer improve their script with minimal confusion or stress, and also, hopefully, make it a gratifying experience. They will provide well-thought-through notes in a respectful, practical and attentive way, without involving their egos, keeping the writer and the story their top priority.

A script editor is not, at least when they are script editing, a writer. They do not write, or rewrite; they provide feedback, guidance, encouragement and constructive criticism. They are not there to come up with the story, but to get the very best out of a writer in the same way a coach or mentor would. Their job is to manage writers and ensure they stay focused and adhere to the project's brief.

Script editors can come on board at any point during the process. Often they are hired directly by the writer to discuss and organise ideas, outlines, story and character arcs or any other elements the writer wishes to have help with prior to a draft being written. They

13

sometimes begin later in the process, frequently just as the first draft is completed and prior to the submission process, providing the writer with a safe and objective assessment of the script along with suggestions for improvements.

They are regularly hired on behalf of a producer, a production company, a commissioner, or a writing team to assist the writer and the script during its development. There are no rules as to when the script editor joins the team, but whenever they do, their job is to support the writer and the script and assist in getting it ready for production.

On a long-running television show the job requires added skills as each show has its own way of working and the script editor becomes a vital link between the writers and the show's producers. A script editor on a television show is a member of the production team and has many responsibilities, including finding new writing talent, working with script writers developing storyline and series ideas, and ensuring that scripts are suitable for production. The script editor will work closely with the writer at each draft of the script, giving the writer feedback on the quality of their work, helping them meet the needs of the project, ensuring that the writing reflects the style, tone and nature of the show, and suggesting improvements where needed. They will make sure the practical issues of the show, such as show continuity and running time (length of the show), are maintained. Unlike the writers, script editors will usually be full-time members of the production team, working closely with the producer.

No matter what the genre, the format or the content, the objective and challenge during the script development journey is always the same – creating a workable draft while supporting the writer and producer's vision. The intention of this book is to provide information and tools required for the journey.

RESPONSIBILITIES OF A SCRIPT EDITOR

The script editor's job is to read and analyse the script –
give clear and strong notes and help the writer find
their best version of the script.

WHAT SKILLS DOES A SCRIPT EDITOR NEED?

Having a passion for storytelling is a prerequisite for anyone in development, and that is even truer for script editors. Script editors must immerse themselves in stories, read loads of screenplays and books, watch plenty of films, and see tons of theatre. They must virtually dive inside a story and examine it from all angles, so it is crucial that they love reading, love watching stories unfold, and are highly knowledgeable about how storytelling and film structure work.

A script editor is comparable to an auto-mechanic. An auto-mechanic has to know how a car works in order to help customers care, repair, or maintain a vehicle. They are knowledgeable about all kinds of makes, years and styles of cars and they understand how cars are built and operate. In the same way, a script editor has to know how stories work, how they are built, in order to help writers successfully craft them.

Script editors must be diplomats, tactful, responsive and respectful. They must be good listeners and enjoy working with people. Having good communication skills is essential. Script editors must be able to substantiate their opinions with valid arguments within the context of the filmmaking process, and their opinions should be focused on assisting screenwriters and producers realise the potential of their screenplays. They must be able to communicate clearly, both in writing and in conversation, their thoughts, criticisms and opinions about the work and be able to provide clear, objective opinions and give detailed explanations of their reasoning. A script editor must always remember that they are there to help the writer find their own answers... not to tell them how to write their story.

Script editors must understand the numerous development stages a project will undergo with regard to its particular format, and be aware of the different ways that genre and writing style affect an audience. They must be proficient in the crafting of a strong synopsis and premise line, as well as evaluating the contents required in a reader's script report including: the structure, tone, character, plot, action, dialogue, genre and style of the writing. Equally important is the use of dramatic tools, such as dramatic tension, irony, viewpoint, and suspense.

The best script editors provide their clients with diverse perspectives on their work, ensuring the writers consider the varied ways an audience might view the story while also considering the potential commercial market for the film. They should stay abreast of the current trends in production, incorporating into their reports an appraisal of how the project might fare in the intended market.

A script editor should continually be meeting and working with writers, developing a list of talent they respect and want to work with. Part of a script editor's value is their knowledge of and relationships with screenwriters. A script editor must stay knowledgeable about the current and available writing talent, which means reading script after script, keeping abreast of films and television shows and actively looking for new writing talent. It also means developing relationships with literary agents so that, when a broadcaster, independent film or TV company, or a producer, asks for suggestions about screenwriting talent for a project, they are able to provide strong ones.

For a television series, a script editor is also responsible for making sure that the logic and continuity of each script and story is maintained. As there are regularly numerous writers on a continuing series, and multiple stories being developed at a time, the script editor is often the only person available who knows the details of the show's 'bible' (history), and to a large degree the responsibility for story consistency falls upon them.

Strong negotiation and interpersonal skills are required to navigate through the development process and a script editor must be capable of liaising effectively among writers, researchers, producers and development executives. They must mediate effectively between the screenwriter's creative ideas and the requirements of the project. Helping the writer stay focused on the agreed nature of the work and aware of the kind of film that producers and financiers expect to be delivered is essential.

To work effectively, script editors must be present at all script development meetings to ensure that all parties share the same vision for the project, keeping a record of all notes and decisions made.

Script editors can be hired at any point of the development process, even well before a script has been written. A writer might hire them directly for creative support, or they might be brought on board by a producer, a development team or production company.

Making a film or television show is an expensive venture. Time and money are critical factors and production companies and producers cannot afford to waste either.

Script editing can vary enormously depending on the writer's personality and needs, and on the type of project being done. For example, developing original material is very different to working within an existing series or on commissioned work. Original work is a very creative process. Writers often need help clarifying their ideas and shaping their sense of story and characters. To that end, writers will often engage a script editor in the early stages of the process to discuss ideas, and help map out or outline their projects.

MOST IMPORTANTLY:
A good script editor never imposes their ideas onto a project,
but helps the writer cultivate their own ideas.

Script editors are hired to energise, motivate, and help writers tell the stories that are meaningful to them in a way that connects with their intended audience. It is also essential to help writers find ways to tell their stories in a format and style that is likely to be commissioned. There is no foolproof formula for success, but the odds greatly increase for writers who are clear about the story they are telling, know who they are writing for, and how best to reach their intended audience.

STORYTELLING AND SCREENPLAY
STRUCTURE

Although this is not a book about screenwriting or story structure, understanding the building blocks of script construction is absolutely necessary for a script editor, and frankly essential for anyone in development at all, including script readers.

It's important to be aware that writers, especially experienced ones, will have their own methods of organising their work and so it's not helpful – or, in fact, the script editor's place – to try to change or impose ways of working onto them. Instead it is important that script editors be knowledgeable about the many different ways in which a screenwriter might approach their work so as to be able to adapt accordingly.

Screenplay paradigms exist to guide and support a writer's existing story. The story idea should come <u>first</u>, before the application of any method. Methods only exist to support the story, and writers should be encouraged to break the rules if it will strengthen their script.

STRUCTURE

I realise that the word 'structure' can sound very intimidating, but it shouldn't. Structure is the spine of the story, meaning how the script is built and the way in which the parts of the script function together.

Structure is the escalation of conflict,
the cause and effect of events in a story.

A script editor must understand the nature of screenplays, and the effect that different types of narratives and genres will have on audiences. They must be able to give objective opinions about the writing and provide detailed explanations of their comments and reasoning, offering effective guidance on how to resolve any problems.

There are many theories on screenplay structure and I recommend that anyone interested in script development read up on, and become familiar with, as many as possible. As with any creative form, there are numerous schools of thought, all with valid points of view and valuable insights and tools. Which method (if any) a writer chooses to use is an individual preference, and irrelevant in terms of the final outcome. What is important is that a script editor be knowledgeable about the different forms, and able to work and communicate within them. Simply put, it helps if you and the writer speak the same language and use terminology that you both clearly understand.

Personally, I do not suggest that a writer limit themself to any set of rules or any one paradigm. It is a wholly personal decision. Trying to force a specific form can be very constraining and the writer has to work within their comfort zone. However, I do believe that understanding the components of story structure can also be very liberating, and can in many ways give the writer greater freedom, as well as saving them precious writing time. Nevertheless, writers must acquire their own practice and it's up to the script editor to be informed and adaptable to meet their needs.

We will now move on to a brief overview of the structure of storytelling and screenplay writing. *Please note that, as we discuss the different components of the work, various terminologies will crop up and I will do my best to explain these as we go along. I have also included a glossary of terms at the back of this book.*

BRIEF OVERVIEW

Storytelling has been essential since the dawn of humankind and is one of the most important things that we do. Story gives us history, perspective, the ability to share our knowledge, to process experiences, to dream, and so much more.

So, how do stories work?

First, we have to have a storyteller. That is a vital role and the storyteller must have something to say. Whether the story is simply for entertainment value or contains a message or moral, the storyteller – that is, the writer – must have something they want to convey.

I know this sounds obvious – but you'd be surprised how frequently scripts get written without the writer having a clear idea what it is they really want to say.

Stories require characters. Characters are usually people, but they can also be animals or any number of other creatures or beings, even inanimate objects. Most of us have seen animation films where the characters are not human, but are nevertheless vital characters (think of the teapot in *Beauty and the Beast* or the Hal 9000 computer in *2001: A Space Odyssey*).

In the story at least one of the characters must take a journey. The type of journey that the character takes – be it physical or emotional – is what defines what kind of story (genre) it is, and how the story will be organised. It is also crucial that the audience cares, empathises or can identify with the main character in some way.

Most stories involve some kind of change – and how the character copes with change is what defines them. Equally important is *conflict*. Conflict is the reason people engage in stories. Without conflict (a struggle or battle) there is no story, but simply a series of events.

Stories need to be organised or structured in a way that gives the audience everything they need to know when they need to know it, while also keeping them interested in finding out what happens next. The most prevalent theory of screenplay structure is the **three-act structure** based on the three-act paradigm, inspired by Aristotle's *Poetics*. This structure is based on the observation that all stories have a beginning, middle and end.

It is true that, often, screenplay timelines are manipulated and jumbled, but even so they contain a beginning, middle and end, and although there are successful writers and teachers who rebuff this approach, there is still no denying that it is, and has been, the most prevalent method to date.

In its simplest terms the three-act structure breaks down into: act one – the beginning (the set-up); act two – the middle (conflict/confrontation); and act three – the end (the resolution).

These three acts correlate to the audience's emotional experience. In the beginning, the audience is introduced to the characters and becomes emotionally involved with them. During the middle, the emotional commitment is strengthened by rising tension and expectation. The end brings the audience's emotional involvement to a reasonable and (hopefully) satisfying conclusion.

THE THREE-ACT STRUCTURE IN GREATER DETAIL

ACT ONE – THE SET-UP

Act one is the beginning – it's where the story takes off. It introduces the main character(s) and the world they live in and answers the questions who, what, where, when and how. It deals with location, setting and tone, presenting the main character's goal and the story question.

In act one we learn about the character(s), see them in action and discover what their situation is, what they are up against and what motivates them. Here we also learn what skills they have and what they lack.

The main character (also known as the *protagonist*) is usually troubled or flawed. Their need or flaw is present from the very beginning of the story, but they lack the ability, desire or need to change. They are usually stuck in their situation and are unable to change until they are forced to.

The set-up culminates in a dynamic on-screen event that incites the characters' desire/need to take action. This on-screen event is known as the **inciting incident** and is what kick-starts the story.

ACT 1 Rising Action	ACT 2 Rising Action	ACT 3 Falling Action
· Beginning – Life as it was… · Set up – Story question. · Inciting Incident/Catalyst · Call to Action/Adventure · Turning point · Climax ACT ONE	· End of the beginning – beginning of the Middle · Life torn apart · Obstacles · Confrontation · First culmination · Midpoint – Big Twist – Turning point. · Trials/obstacles/disaster/crisis · Inciting incident (Hook) · Plot point	· End – Falling Action. · Life Renewed – for better or worse. · Climax. The Final Battle. · Showdown. · Wrap up. · Denouement
Notes · Strong opening Image · Strong opening Scene · State the Theme · Introduce characters / Introduce the problem · Establish point of view, genre, style etc. · Establish main character's situation, and the premise. · Show what needs to change. · First Problem – meet supporting characters/antagonist · Debate and find a solution · Solution doesn't work or disappears – added conflict and problem worsens · Life will never be the same.	**Notes** · Moral dilemma and doubt. · Will protagonist get what is needed? · Seek a new way · Obstacle · Obstacle – stakes intensify	**Notes** · Outcome – win or Lose? · Story question Answered. · No going back – what will the future bring? · Letting go of the emotional battle – facing reality. · Denouement · Final Risk · Resolution. · Final Image · Tag or bridge if necessary

The inciting incident is the moment when the dramatic conflict is presented. It's the first pronouncement of the predicament to come, and is usually delivered in a very visual and formidable way.

An inciting incident generally happens in one of the following ways:

- **A new and critical piece of information is given to the main character.**

  For example, *The Doctor* is a film about a successful and arrogant heart surgeon who learns the value of life after he develops a life-threatening illness that forces him to be a patient.

  The inciting incident is the moment the doctor discovers that he, himself, is ill.

- **An event forces the main character into conflict.**

  For example, in *The Impossible*, we are shown a happy family on vacation; then a tsunami strikes.

  The tsunami striking is the inciting incident.

- **A series of small events accumulates and forces the main character on a journey.**

  In *Planes, Trains and Automobiles*, Neal Page, a high-strung executive, tries to get home for Thanksgiving dinner, but events accumulate that prevent him from being able to travel easily, and he is forced on a life-changing trip with Del Griffith, a homeless shower-curtain-ring salesman.

  The inciting incident in *Planes, Trains and Automobiles* is that Neal's flight is cancelled and he must find an alternative way to get home for Thanksgiving.

As you can see, the inciting incident significantly changes the characters' life and story. That is the moment the story really begins.

The inciting incident sparks two important questions:

- What does the character need?
- What is preventing them from getting it?

These two questions define what the conflict of the story is.

In *Jaws*, what does Sheriff Brody (the main character) need?
To save his community from the killer shark.

What is preventing him from doing that?
His boss, the mayor, won't allow him to close the beach.

The characters' attempts to deal with the inciting incident lead to a second and more dramatic situation, known as the **first turning point**.

The first turning point is where the main character is shoved deeper into the heart of the story and realises there is no turning back. It signals the end of the first act and ensures life will never be the same again for the character. It also raises a **dramatic question** that will be answered in the climax of the film.

The first turning point of *Thelma and Louise* comes when Louise shoots a man who is on the verge of raping Thelma. This action completely changes the course of the story. Up until then, Thelma and Louise have been on a recreational road trip, taking a break from their tedious lives; but when Thelma kills the man, they become criminals and everything changes.

The dramatic question is usually directed in terms of the protagonist's call to action. For example, in *Jaws* – will Sheriff Brody kill the great white shark and save his community? Or in *The Matrix* – will Neo face the challenges of the Matrix and accept that he is the one? In *The Impossible* – will the family survive the devastating tsunami? Will Neal Page make it home for Thanksgiving? Will Thelma and Louise get their normal lives back?

The answer to the dramatic question is not always a 'yes'. Sometimes the power of a story is that the answer is 'no'.

By the end of the first act two things must be accomplished:

- The protagonist must be deeply rooted in the conflict that prevents them from getting what they want/need and must be fully committed to their journey.

- The audience must be engaged in their predicament and know what is at stake in the story.

ACT TWO – THE DEVELOPMENT/CONFRONTATION (THE MIDDLE)

Act two tends to give writers the most trouble. It is the longest of the three acts and is difficult to get right, but it is also the heart of the film. It contains the end of the beginning and the beginning of the end of the story, and must progress logically. Act two is where the essential action (drama, battles or romance) takes place and where we are given (shown) what has been promised in act one. For this reason, act two is also sometimes called the confrontation.

In act two the relationships introduced in act one are further developed and they should contribute to the main action, whether they help or hinder the protagonist. As the plot intensifies, further complexities are also presented and the protagonist struggles to reach their goal or overcome the obstacles/conflicts that stand in their way. Act two is generally propelled by the main character's decision to take action and it's where the consequences of that decision start to unfold.

As the protagonist attempts to resolve the problem initiated by the first turning point, they find that the situation progressively worsens. The character has not yet acquired the skills to deal with the obstacles that confront them and must learn new skills and gain a higher sense of self-awareness in order to resolve their predicament.

The second act is usually divided into two parts delineated by the **midpoint**. The midpoint is another turning point that again increases the stakes, either by making it even more difficult for the character to get what they need or by making it more important that they do. The midpoint is often referred to as a **reversal** because it forces the main character to create a new plan. What they were doing isn't working and whatever way they were planning to resolve the situation is disrupted and becomes no longer an option. The obstacles have intensified or the antagonist (rival/opponent/enemy) has increased the pressure.

As the stakes escalate, it becomes even more difficult for the main character to get what they want and need. If they are indecisive or confused about what to do then something must happen by the midpoint of the script to make their new goal clear. The main character will often attempt to return to the world from which they came, but will discover that there is no going back, and that they must face the conflict in order to progress.

In *Thelma and Louise*, the two protagonists realise that, with the police on their tail, they cannot return home and live a normal life. They have to keep running, and so they drive towards Mexico.

In *Jaws*, the midpoint comes when the mayor refuses to close the beach for the Fourth of July weekend and Brody's son just barely escapes being attacked. These events raise the stakes for Brody and motivate him to force the mayor to hire Sam Quint to hunt and kill the shark.

> *Throughout the second act the character's problem must*
> *continue to escalate as the story action intensifies.*

At the end of act two (the second-act break) there is a **second turning point** – a pivotal moment when the story once again changes direction and the stakes are increased. The story should again state the dramatic question.

For *Jaws* – will Brody ensure that the shark is killed and save the community?

Sometimes a time limit, or ticking clock, is introduced. All seems lost for the protagonist – it's their lowest point – until new information propels them towards the climactic conclusion.

ACT THREE - RESOLUTION (THE END)

Balance is restored. Act three must provide clear scenes/events that build to the climax, delivering a resolution. In act three the main character's story and all subplots should be resolved and the dramatic story question should be answered.

This act is usually the shortest in length and it is where the required confrontation between the opposing forces takes place.

27

Here the main character is face to face with the villain and the final showdown ensues.

The climax is the scene or sequence where the main tensions of the story are brought to their most intense point and where the dramatic question is answered.

The resolution leaves the protagonist with a new sense of themselves, who they really are, what they can accomplish, and also gives the audience an understanding of what the importance and meaning of the journey has been.

CHARACTER + WANT/NEED + OBSTACLES = STORY

- The character must have an extreme want or need.
- Their goal should be difficult, but ultimately possible to achieve.
- The story should be about a character that the audience can care about.
- The story should create full emotional impact and audience connection.
- The story should come to a satisfying conclusion – even if it's not a happy ending.

THE BUILDING BLOCKS - SCENES

Scenes are the building blocks of all screenplays. Each scene should include the answers to: who, what, where, when and why.

- Who – which character or characters are involved?
- What – what is the circumstance or obstacles?
- Where – what is the location; where is everything happening?
- When – when is the scene occurring? (Time of day and/or time reference needed to follow the story.)
- Why – what is the purpose of the characters' actions? Why are they doing it?

Scenes are composed of:

- SCENE HEADINGS: List the location and time of the scene.

- ACTION LINES: State what is being revealed visually; what will be seen as you enter a scene. This establishes the setting, situation and event.

- CHARACTER NAMES: Inform the reader who is speaking (names should be typed in all caps).

- DIALOGUE: What are the characters saying?

The three-act paradigm is a fundamental method that is widely accepted. It is very broad, allowing for countless story variations within it. Studies have shown that this pattern – beginning, middle and end – appeals to our human nature because it mirrors the natural way the human mind processes and attempts to rationalise and resolve information. In other words, human beings process information by using the same pattern, the sequence of having a beginning, middle and end.

There are, however, some who reject this form, claiming it is a construct imposed by the Hollywood film industry. However, most do recognise that it has worth as a basic root of storytelling. Their argument is that it is too basic and that it encourages writers to be mechanical and produce formulaic and episodic scripts. But that can be true of any of the theories, and you will find that the vast majority of scripts, even those written by writers who reject this method, can ultimately be broken down into a three-act structure.

'All stories should have a beginning, a middle and an end, but not necessarily in that order.' – Jean-Luc Godard

For better or worse, the three-act structure has kept the film industry afloat for the last century. It is an effective and useful way to begin looking at story.

STORY STRUCTURE FORMS

There are many other story structure forms available and I suggest you become familiar with as many as possible. John Yorke, Syd Field, Linda Seger, Linda Aronson, Christopher Booker, Michael Hauge,

Joseph Campbell, Blake Snyder and Robert McKee are some of the most popular teachers out there and each has ideas well worth studying. For the purposes of this book, I have included a brief summary of the four-act structure, the five-act structure, sequencing, Blake Snyder's beat sheet, and John Truby's seven steps of story anatomy. These provide valuable ways of looking at the elements of story and hopefully this will inspire you to continue exploring.

THE FOUR-ACT STRUCTURE

The four-act structure is basically the same as the three-act structure except that the second act has now been divided into two. It breaks down like this:

ACT ONE

- The introduction and inciting incident/hook happen.
- The initial stakes – what the main character wants/needs – are established.
- Something happens to up the stakes (the lock-in).

ACT TWO

- The hero (or heroine) comes up with a plan to solve the problem or get what they want. (If this is a murder mystery, they find out who the murderer is.)
- They put the plan into action.
- The plan fails. Everything the hero and his companions thought they knew turns out to be wrong and they are forced to go back to square one.

ACT THREE

- The hero recovers from the events of act two and tries to come up with a new approach.
- Things keep getting worse for the hero and his companions. The opposing force increases.

- The stakes are raised.
- By the end of act three it seems as though the hero has lost.

ACT FOUR

- The hero comes up with a new plan.
- The hero solves the problem.
- The hero achieves their goal (finds the murderer, etc).
- Equilibrium is restored.

THE FIVE-ACT STRUCTURE

The five-act structure is also a modification of the three-act structure. It breaks down like this:

ACT ONE: INTRODUCTION OR EXPOSITION

The exposition is where your main characters and themes are introduced and where the world in which the action takes place is established. Here you must also introduce any and all thematic elements that are going to resonate throughout the story, as well as any problems or goals your protagonist is facing.

Conflicts and themes must be established before the action takes off and should be directed towards the dramatic tension of the story. As we know, themes vary greatly from one story to another – whether the script is about the futility of war, the trappings of power, or the notion that love conquers all, the ideology at the heart of the story must be ignited from the very beginning.

ACT TWO: COMPLICATION OR RISING ACTION

In act two, the basic conflict escalates and the course of action becomes more complicated. Obstacles and secondary conflicts are introduced to keep our protagonist from reaching his or her goal.

Remember that the antagonist is not always a character – it might be a disease, substance abuse, or an act of nature, such as a tsunami.

ACT THREE: CLIMAX (CLIMAX OF ACTION)

The development of the climax reaches its highest point and the protagonist reaches a crossroads that will lead them to either defeat or victory.

Also known as the turning point, the climax marks a notable change, for better or worse, in the protagonist's journey. This point begins act three, accelerating the events your character must experience before their story is resolved.

With tragedy, the protagonist begins the story on top of the world before everything begins to unravel, while comedies generally do the opposite.

This is where the bulk of the action and drama takes place.

ACT FOUR: FALLING ACTION

During the falling action, the conflict between the protagonist and antagonist finally comes to a head, and a winner is determined.

Often, the main character experiences a 'false victory' or 'false defeat' that gets turned on its head, providing a story surprise. Usually a 'false victory' is followed by a final defeat, while a 'false defeat' is followed with a true victory. (Think of how many times you have seen a villain seemingly dead, then come back to fight another round before the final defeat.)

This falling action also often contains a final moment of suspense, keeping the final outcome in doubt until the resolution.

ACT FIVE: RESOLUTION

The conflict is resolved. Resolution ties up all the loose ends and concludes the story. The characters return to normalcy, and the viewer experiences an emotional catharsis (release).

In traditional comedies, the resolution leaves the main character better off than they started, while traditional tragedies end with the downfall of the hero.

Remember: a good script provides an entertaining and emotional ride – it should have plenty of surprises with well thought through twists and turns. Every positive action, emotion or event your protagonist experiences must be followed with an equally strong negative action, emotion or event.

SEQUENCE METHOD

The next method that I will introduce is the sequence method, which has its origins in the time when films were set up on multiple reels, causing interruptions to the story. Screenwriters wrote in cliffhangers at the end of each reel in order to keep the audience interested while the next reel was being set up. It has since become a very useful tool for organising a story.

The general idea is that a screenplay can be written in sequences of about 15 pages each, and by focusing on solving the dramatic aspects of each of these sequences in detail, a writer can more easily construct the script as a whole. In other words, it may be easier to write a bunch of shorter sequences than have to think of the film as one long one.

Sequencing can be broken down in multiple ways, but typically in a feature film there are eight sections. This tool can be used on its own or as a supplement to the other structures.

Each sequence is like a 'chapter' comprising a collection of scenes and punctuated by a reversal at the end. This technique works best if there is a goal or mini-goal in each sequence that ends with a cliffhanger. The writer should lay all eight sequences out and write the objective for their protagonist within each one. Each of these eight objectives will drive the story forward until the next sequence arrives. In addition to listing the goal of the character in each sequence, it helps if the writer lists the purpose of the sequence itself, giving a breakdown of where they want the sequence to go, as well as any other detailed ideas they have.

SEQUENCE 1 - INCITING INCIDENT/STATUS QUO

- Establish the world of the story and the hero's problem or unease with the world (their need).

- The sequence ends with the inciting incident that threatens to change everything.

SEQUENCE 2 - LOCKED-IN

- The hero is called to action – they may refuse the call, but by the end of the sequence they are locked-in to the adventure and have passed the point of no return.

- In this sequence, they try to solve the problem the easy way, but fail.

SEQUENCE 3 - RAISING THE STAKES

- Now that the character is locked-in, they face their first challenge in the new world. The stakes have been raised now that they are locked-in. The exploration of the new world occurs here, and the characters of the new world are introduced here as well. This sequence is about exploration and playing out the concept.

- This is the first time the hero tries in earnest to solve the problem.

SEQUENCE 4 - MIDPOINT

- The midpoint is a collection of scenes including the preparation and aftermath of a huge event that is either a false defeat or false victory for the protagonist.

SEQUENCE 5 - RISING ACTION

- The stakes are raised as the obstacles/villains close in on the hero. The character finally begins to grow in this sequence, and subplots are played out along with the minor characters' arcs.

- At the end of this sequence there's a new way to solve the problem.

SEQUENCE 6 – ALL IS LOST

- This sequence reframes the entire film with a twist that changes everything. Hope is crushed and the bad guys move in; the hero faces their greatest fear.

SEQUENCE 7 – NEW TENSION AND TWIST

- The inciting incident is resolved, the hero defeats the enemy, gets the girl, and sometimes an additional twist can be placed here.

SEQUENCE 8 – RESOLUTION

- This is the closing image, where the character resolves the final conflict. This is usually one to two scenes long, but can be shortened.

The advantages of the sequence method are that it:

- Breaks the screenplay into manageable chunks;
- Works well in conjunction with the three-act structure and the beat structure;
- Helps focus plot points and eliminate those that aren't valuable or necessary.

THE BLAKE SNYDER BEAT SHEET

This is a very popular method created by Blake Snyder, author of *Save the Cat!*

Opening Image – an image that sets the tone, mood and style of the story. Also represents the struggle – a snapshot of the main character's problem, before the adventure begins.

Theme Stated – in the first five minutes (during the set-up) – what your story is about; the message, the truth. Usually, a question posed or statement made to the main character, or in their presence, but they don't understand the truth – and won't until they have some personal experience and context to support it.

Set-up – the first ten pages. Expand on the 'before' snapshot. Present the main character's world as it is, and what is missing in their life. Plant all characters' ties and character behaviours that need to be addressed in the story.

Catalyst – the moment where life as it is changes. Getting fired, finding you only have a month to live, a telegram arriving or the phone ringing with news of a loved one's death, catching your partner cheating, allowing a monster into your house, meeting the love of your life, etc. The 'before' world is no more; change is underway.

Debate – this is the last chance the hero has to back out, and for a moment, or a brief number of moments, the main character resists/ rejects the journey they must make. They are riddled with questions – can I face this challenge? Do I have what it takes? Should I give up? In the end they realise they have no choice – and a bigger question emerges as to whether they can succeed now that they have been forced into the situation.

Break into Two (act break) – the main character makes the important choice and the journey begins. We leave the old world and enter the new and challenging 'upside-down' world of act two.

B Story – the B story gives the audience a breather. It is a parallel (usually minor) storyline that supports, discusses and strengthens the theme, and provides nuggets of truth that help the A story. The B story is important, as it provides layers and depth.

The Promise of the Premise – this is the fun part of the story, where we see what the idea is about. It's the core and essence of the movie poster. This is where Jim Carrey in *Bruce Almighty* gets to play God; it's when Bruce Willis in *Die Hard* first outsmarts the villains. It's when the main character explores the new world they have entered and the audience is entertained by the premise they have been promised.

Midpoint – is the middle of the story. At the midpoint everything is either 'great' or 'awful' and the stakes are raised. (Getting everything they want at the midpoint is usually a false victory for the character, and having everything be awful at the midpoint is usually a false defeat.) Depending on the story, the midpoint must be the opposite of the finale/resolution.

Bad Guys Close In – doubt, jealousy, fear, enemies, both physical and emotional, regroup to defeat the main character's goal, and the main character's 'great'/'awful' situation disintegrates.

All is Lost – the opposite moment from the midpoint, when the main character realises they've lost everything, and that what they thought was awful/great has an alternative meaning. The initial goal/need now looks even more impossible to achieve than before. Something changes or someone dies, and it can be physical or emotional, but the change clears the way for something new to begin.

Dark Night of the Soul – the darkness before the dawn. The main character hits rock bottom and mourns the loss of what has changed or died – the dream, the goal, a loved one, etc. They feel utterly defeated and this is also the moment just before the hero reaches deep down inside and pulls out the last and best idea that will save them, and everyone around them. (They don't have the idea yet, but are about to pick themselves up, and try again).

Break Into Three (the solution) – thanks to a new idea, fresh inspiration, or last-minute thematic advice from the B story (usually the love interest), the main character chooses to try again.

Finale – the wrap-up. Lessons learned are now applied. This time around, the main character triumphs because they incorporate the theme – and the truth now makes sense to them. They have advanced in their fight for the goal because they have experience from the A story and context from the B story. Act three is about synthesis.

Final Image – the opposite of the opening image, proving, visually, that a change has occurred within the character and that it's real.

THE SEVEN KEY STEPS OF STORY ANATOMY

The final method I am going to present comes from John Truby, one of Hollywood's premier screenwriting instructors and story consultants. Truby's book *The Anatomy of Story* is very popular and one that should definitely be on your 'to read' list. In it he proposes that every good story is founded on seven dramatic steps: problem/need, desire, opponent, plan, battle, self-revelation, and new equilibrium. These steps he explains are the same steps that all humans must work through in order to solve a life problem.

1. PROBLEM AND NEED

- The main character must want or need something.

- From the beginning, the hero of the story has something holding them back, something missing in their life that is so deep, it is ruining their life.

- Their need is what the hero must realise within themselves in order to progress and it usually involves overcoming weaknesses, changing, or growing in some way.

- Their need is what sets up every other step of the story.

- Heroes should have a moral need as well as a psychological need.

- A moral need is a flaw that hurts others. A psychological need is a flaw that hurts only the hero.

- The hero should not be aware of their need at the beginning of the story, but becomes aware near the end, after having gone through the journey (the story) and much pain and/or struggle.

2. DESIRE

Once the hero's weakness and need have been established, they must also be given a desire. The hero's desire is a separate element from what the hero needs. Their desire is their particular aim or goal in the story, and it is the driving force of the narrative. Their desire is the element on which everything else in the story hangs.

To clarify:

- Need has to do with the hero overcoming a weakness within themselves.

- Desire is a goal outside of the character.

- Once the hero has their desire, they move in a direction and take actions to reach their goal.

Desire is on the surface and gives the audience something to root for – it's what the audience thinks the story is about. Underneath that, hidden away, is the bigger picture – what the character needs and how they must change in order to have a better life.

3. OPPONENT

- The opponent, or antagonist, is the character who wants to keep the protagonist/hero from getting what they want. A true opponent not only wants to prevent the hero from achieving their desire but is also competing with the hero for the same goal.

- The trick to creating an opponent who wants the same goal as the hero is to discover what their deepest conflict is.

- Decide – what is the most important thing they are fighting about? That must be the focus of the story.

4. PLAN

- Action stems from a plan. The plan is the strategy that the hero will use to overcome the opponent and obstacles to reach their goal. It is linked to both desire and to the opponent; the plan should always focus on defeating the opponent and reaching the goal.

5. BATTLE

- The battle is the final conflict between the hero and the opponent and determines who will reach their goal and win. The final battle may be a conflict of actions or it may be a conflict of words.

6. SELF-REVELATION

- The battle is over. It has been intense and painful for the hero, but it has also provided a valuable lesson and given them new insight into themselves.

- Self-revelation, has two forms:

  1. A psychological self-revelation. This is where the hero strips away the façade they have lived behind and sees themself honestly for the first time. This stripping away does not come to them easily and it should be the most difficult/courageous act the hero performs in the story.

  2. A moral self-revelation. The hero doesn't just see themself in a new way; they also gain insight about the proper way to treat others. In effect, the hero realises that they have been wrong and have hurt others, and that they must change. They then prove they have changed by taking a new moral action (or actions).

- As a rule, it is better not to have your hero say what they have learned, but to show it through their actions. And remember that the quality of a script is linked to the quality of this self-revelation.

7. NEW EQUILIBRIUM

- Resolution. The hero has moved to a higher or lower level as a result of going through the journey. Except now there is a fundamental and permanent change in their character.

- If the self-revelation is positive, the hero realises who they truly are and learns how to live properly in the world, moving to a higher level.

- If the hero has a negative revelation, learning they have committed a terrible crime that expresses a corrupt personal flaw, or is incapable of having a self-revelation, the hero falls or is destroyed.

The components in each of these forms have great similarities in spite of the different terminology and varied designs. Ultimately, these forms are simply maps to help writers get where they are trying to go, and it doesn't matter which map they use as long as they reach their destination. It's like having a bunch of different recipes for the same dish; it's up to the chef to decide which one to use – if any. They may pick one, mix and match or invent their own; it doesn't matter. All that does matter is how the script turns out, and if the structure and story are effective.

However, from a script editor's point of view, it's important to know any of the references a writer might use, so cultivating a deep and expansive understanding of all of the available views on structure and terminology will only benefit you. To that end, I have included a suggested reading list, which is at the back of this book. Do plenty of research so that you are equipped to work effectively with writers who adhere to the various practices. Don't be surprised if writers mix and match terms and phrases; just make sure that you are speaking the same language as you go about the work.

> 'All notions of paradigms and foolproof story models for commercial success are nonsense. Anxious, inexperienced writers obey rules. Rebellious, unschooled writers break rules. Artists master the form.' – Robert McKee

THE PRINCIPLES OF **GENRE**

Genre is a term used to categorise the style, organisation and nature of a story. Film genres have recurring and recognisable patterns and conventions that define their construction. Each includes one or more of the following: content and subject matter, themes, mood, settings and props, period, plot, central narrative events, ideas, styles, structures, situations, icons, characters and sometimes celebrity.

There is no official manual of genre definitions. You will find that if you read a dozen books, there will be a dozen different ways in which genre is defined and broken down. It is not a fixed or exact form, and films often overlap several genres, creating variations and hybrids. Genres will also change and evolve in response to social and historical circumstances; they can go out of fashion, and undergo transformation over time. Therefore, there will always be alternative views raised in any discussion about how to classify film genre.

The point of genre is not to limit or pigeonhole a story, but to identify and understand the emotional landscapes of it. There has been a great deal of research done on determining how audiences select which films they will go and see, and genre has proved a strong influence. One of the main reasons people gave for not going to see a film was because they were unclear what the genre was. In other words, they didn't know what the film was about and couldn't tell if they'd like it or not – and so decided not to go and see it. This is why genre is so regularly used in marketing and promoting a film.

Genre answers the question – what are the expectations an audience will have when seeing this kind of story?

Here is a look at various genre and subgenre forms:

ACTION

The primary element in these films is the physical action. They are high-energy, big-budget films with stunts, chases, battles, escapes, non-stop motion, spectacular rhythm and pacing, all designed for pure audience escapism. The action hero generally wins in the end.

Examples: *Mission Impossible*, the Bond films, *Speed*, *Taken*, *Mad Max*

ADVENTURE

Adventure films are also action-packed and usually revolve around some kind of quest – such as finding treasure. They are typically set in exotic locales. Action and adventure are so intertwined that they are often treated as one. Some subgenres are spy and espionage films, superhero films, disaster/survival films, treasure hunts, epics and some fantasy films.

Examples: *Pirates of the Caribbean*, *Raiders of the Lost Ark*, *Romancing the Stone*, *Jurassic World*, *Tomorrowland*

BUDDY FILM

The plot of a buddy film revolves around the friendship between two protagonists.

Examples: *Dumb and Dumber*, *Ghost World*, *Romy and Michele's High School Reunion*, *The Odd Couple*, *Midnight Run*, *21 Jump Street*

CHILDREN

Aimed at entertaining young audiences, many of these films are educational and demonstrate a moral message.

Examples: the Care Bears films, and the Rugrats movies, *Parent Trap*

COMEDY

Comedies are generally for pure entertainment. They have light-hearted plots designed to provoke laughter with jokes and by exaggerating the situation, action, language and relationships of the characters.

Comedy is often intermingled with other genres. One of the most important rules of comedy writing is that no one really gets hurt. The only exception is in black comedy, where the scale often tips towards laughs of discomfort. This category also includes screwball comedies, satires, mockumentaries, slapstick, spoofs and parodies.

Examples: *The Hangover*, *The Devil Wears Prada*, *Meet the Parents*, *Ted*

Dark comedy/black comedy has dark, edgy subject matter that is treated in a comedic manner.

Examples: *Harold and Maude*, *Heathers*, *Election*

When you add romance to the mix you get the romantic comedy.

Examples: *When Harry Met Sally*, *Midnight in Paris*, *The Wedding Singer*, *Man Up*

When you add drama to the mix you get the subgenre known as dramedy.

Examples: *Up in the Air*, *Spanglish*, *Igby Goes Down*

CRIME/GANGSTER

In crime the main storyline revolves around a crime committed. These films are developed around the menacing actions of criminals or persons who operate outside the law. Criminal and gangster films are often categorised as film noir or detective-mystery films because of underlying similarities between these forms.

This category's many subgenres include murder mystery, detective story, gangster film, film noir, courtroom drama and the thriller.

Examples: *Goodfellas*, *Gone Girl*, *Mystic River*, *Donnie Brasco*

DOCUMENTARY

Films that depict actual persons and real events, made to document an aspect of reality, primarily for the purposes of instruction or maintaining a historical record.

Examples: *Blackfish*, *Roger and Me*, *Enron*, *Amy*

DRAMA

Drama is by far the broadest genre and usually involves intense character development and interaction. This genre is usually broken down into subgenres, which include melodramas, biopics, historical, romantic, and coming-of-age/rites-of-passage dramas.

Drama is generally about a disruption in our lives that causes change and usually has a message of some sort.

Examples: *Black Swan*, *Dallas Buyers Club*, *You Can Count On Me*, *Cake*

Conventions of drama are as follows:

- Exhibits real-life situations with realistic characters, settings and stories

- Portrays journeys of character development

- Intense social interaction

- Purpose of a dramatic storyline is to move the audience emotionally

- Heart of drama is the conflict

- Conflicts include inner/outer realistic struggles that depict hardships, difficulty and pain

- Audience should be able to relate to the characters

- Structured with climaxes and anticlimaxes to keep the audience emotionally attached and the tension ongoing

- A form of realisation at the end

45

A character drama is a story that revolves explicitly around issues of character and is also known as a 'character study' or 'slice of life' drama. These films are usually about a relationship between two people. The story question will be: who are these two people and why do we care about them? What do they want and need?

Examples: *Midnight Cowboy*, *Rain Man*

COMING-OF-AGE/RITES-OF-PASSAGE

These most commonly tend to be films about young people, but in fact a rites-of-passage film can refer to anyone transitioning from one recognisable stage of life to the next (childhood, adolescence, adulthood, marriage, divorce, parenthood, retirement, etc). These stories deal with the struggle of that transition and the main character is taken out of their familiar environment, for example by moving to a new area, starting at a new school, going to war, being forced to retire, etc. There has to be a steep learning curve in the second act, as they struggle with new responsibilities that they didn't previously have. By the end of the story, they have learned a great deal about themselves and learned to live (and flourish) in their new situation. They have grown through their experience, be it subsisting alone in the woods, passing their exams, having to find new ways to occupy their days, or surviving war.

Rites-of-passage and coming-of-age dramas usually have some comic elements.

Examples: *Juno*, *The Perks of Being a Wallflower*, *Almost Famous*, *Great Expectations*, *The Graduate*

COURTROOM OR LEGAL DRAMA

A story revolving around the legal system.

Examples: *The Accused*, *The Verdict*, *A Few Good Men*, *The Rainmaker*

FAMILY DRAMA

These are character-driven and explore strong family relationships. Should have a key reveal about the relationships; something hidden is exposed. The bonds grow closer because of the reveal.

Examples: *Ordinary People*, *American Beauty*, *The Squid and the Whale*, *Boyhood*, *August: Osage County*

EPIC/HISTORICAL/PERIOD

This genre includes costume dramas, historical dramas, war films, biblical, medieval, period films, and the modern epic. These films usually need a large budget, and often cover a large expanse of time set against a vast, panoramic backdrop. These are films about a historical event, real or imagined. (They don't necessarily stick to the naked truth, but they must be faithful to the spirit of the true story.)

Examples: *Ben Hur*, *Lawrence of Arabia*, *The King's Speech*, *Braveheart*

FAMILY

Family films contain appropriate content for younger viewers, but are also geared to entertain parents.

This genre is often blended with others such as animation, comedy and adventure.

Examples: *Paddington*, *Up*, *The Incredibles*, *Frozen*, *Charlie and the Chocolate Factory*

FANTASY

Fantasy films usually take place in a made-up setting where creatures and characters cross the line of reality. In fantasy films the protagonist is often sent on a heroic journey.

Examples: the Harry Potter series, *Lord of the Rings*, *Watchman*, *Star Wars*, *The Avengers*

HORROR

Horror films are designed to frighten. They invoke our hidden fears, and both shock and thrill us at the same time.

Examples: *Let the Right One In*, *The Ring*, *Poltergeist*, *The Shining*, *Evil Dead*, *Carrie*

The subgenres of horror are slasher, teen terror, serial killer, Satanic, and monster films.

LOVE STORY/ROMANCE

The romance plot revolves around the love between two protagonists. It usually contains a theme that explores an issue within love, such as forbidden love, love at first sight, love triangles, and sacrificial love. The tone of romance films can vary greatly. Whether the end is happy or tragic, they aim to evoke strong emotions in the audience.

Examples: *Brokeback Mountain*, *The Notebook*, *Jerry Maguire*, *Love Actually*, *Love Story*

MEMOIR/TRUE STORY/BIOPIC

A film that dramatises the life (or a portion of the life) of an actual person or people.

Examples: *Selma*, *The Social Network*, *Capote*, *The Elephant Man*, *Elizabeth*, *Lincoln*

MUSICAL

Musicals interweave song and dance into the narrative of the film. The songs are used to further the story and give insight into the characters. These films are generally vehicles for escapism and incorporate lavish costumes and sets.

Examples: *The Sound of Music, Grease, Mamma Mia, Into the Woods, Les Miserables*

MYSTERY/SUSPENSE

Mystery and suspense films have similar characteristics and incorporate a strong sense of 'whodunit' in their storylines. They are usually designed to be plausible stories – realistic. A mystery/suspense film focuses on a person trying to solve a mysterious crime. The protagonist investigates, using clues and logical reasoning to unravel the mystery.

Examples: *Chinatown, Insomnia, The Girl with the Dragon Tattoo*

ROAD MOVIE

The most important element of a road movie must be the journey itself. Whether the protagonist is struggling to get away from something like the police, or going towards something like a visit to their ill brother or to compete in a beauty pageant.

Examples: *The Straight Story, Sideways, Little Miss Sunshine, Five Easy Pieces*

SCIENCE FICTION

Brings us technologically advanced worlds in hypothetical futures, filled with stylised science, space ships, extraterrestrial beings and imagined societies. Often, this genre explores the consequence of technological innovation and uses futuristic elements and technologies to explore social, political, and philosophical issues. Science fiction usually contains heroes, villains, unexplored locations, fantastical quests and advanced technology.

Examples: *Interstellar, The Matrix, 2001: A Space Odyssey, Blade Runner, Inception*

SPORTS

Sport films revolve around sport settings, events or athletes. These films frequently have a simple plot that builds up to a significant competitive sporting event. This genre is known for incorporating film techniques to build anticipation and intensity. Sport films have a large range of subgenres, from comedies to dramas, and are more likely than other genres to be based on true-life events.

Examples: *Rocky, Moneyball, The Blind Side, Coach Carter, Bend It Like Beckham*

SUPERNATURAL

These films centre on supernatural elements, such as ghosts, gods and miracles. They explore and emphasise the unknown, and are generally quite suspenseful.

This genre is often crossed with others – creating hybrids like supernatural-comedy and supernatural-fantasy. They often deal with the unknown questions of life and tend to incorporate religious elements.

Examples: *Ghost, Michael, The Ninth Gate, Cocoon, Horns*

THRILLER

Thriller is a genre that revolves around anticipation and suspense. The main character must be under threat and fighting for their survival. These films promote intense excitement, suspense, high-level anticipation, heightened expectation and nerve-wracking tension.

Examples: *The Silence of the Lambs, North by Northwest*

WAR

The plot of a war film revolves around actual combat. War films bring us face to face with the horrors and heartbreak of war and include such themes as heroism, loyalty and human brutality. An anti-war film might emphasise the futility of war, whereas a pro-war film might focus on its gallantry.

Examples: *American Sniper*, *Saving Private Ryan*, *The Deer Hunter*, *Apocalypse Now*

WESTERNS

This genre is defined by its setting – the Wild West of the American frontier. Westerns evoke cowboys, sheriffs, horses and gun fights. Plots often revolve around personal freedom, integrity and the struggle for law and order.

Examples: *Unforgiven*, *3:10 to Yuma*, *The Good, the Bad, and the Ugly*

You should note that many people question whether science-fiction and historical scripts should be considered genres at all. The truth is they are about their distinct settings and need to be combined/ supplemented with another genre in order to demarcate them.

For example, science-fiction and historical genres imply specific production needs, i.e. they take place in specific worlds that need to be defined within the script. In order to know what the audience should expect from the story there needs to be another genre added to the mix. Is it a science-fiction drama? Or comedy? *Interstellar* is a sci-fi drama; *Galaxy Quest* is a sci-fi comedy. Expectations will vary between the two.

The same is true for historical films. Think about *Shakespeare in Love* and *12 Years a Slave*. Both are historical, but very different from each other, and another genre must be added to express what the films really are.

As you become more familiar with genre(s), you will understand how they have been defined and can decide where the boundaries are for yourself.

GENRE AS A DEVELOPMENT TOOL

Genre is simply a way of understanding the basic patterns of a story. Each genre has its own set of rules, its own history, and therefore generates its own set of expectations. Each imposes a convention on story design. So, if you can define the dominant genre in a screenplay, you can work out the expectations raised by that kind of story, which will help serve as a guide through the story development process.

Remember this is a reference only. These conventions are not set in stone. Do not try to force writers to uphold the 'rules', but use them as a reminder of the expectations an audience will have upon viewing a certain type of film, so you can make sure the story satisfies them.

Adhere to the adage, 'Know the rules well, so you can break them effectively!'

The best scripts transcend genre by twisting the beats in ways never seen before. If a writer can satisfy an audience's expectations and somehow still surprise them, their story will feel original and stand out. If an audience is expecting to see one genre but is presented with another, they will most likely be disappointed. That is a reaction that most writers do not wish to get from their audiences. So, if a script is altering genre conventions, it is vitally important that the audience be compensated in a meaningful or clever way. Otherwise, you risk alienating them or losing them entirely.

For instance, in a romantic comedy this is what is expected:

- The story will revolve around two characters (lovers) whom the audience will want, and expect, to see get together at the end.

- The characters don't necessarily need psychological depth and can be defined simply by their current circumstances and situation.

- The pivotal moment, which is when one falls for the other, typically happens in the first act.

- The second act should be full of trials, tribulations and near misses as they fail to get together.

- This is all imbued with humour because it is a comedy.

- The question the audience will ask throughout is: will these two end up together?

The answer is always yes – because in a romantic comedy, there is *always* a happy ending.

But then again... as I've said, there ARE exceptions to every rule. Writers do manipulate and overlap elements of genre, and when it is done well, that usually makes for a unique and unpredictable script. Unpredictability is good – IF the story is satisfying! A great example of a romantic comedy script that successfully altered the rules is *500 Days of Summer*. In it the main characters don't end up together; instead, after all their trials and tribulations, they each learn some tough lessons about love, but end up apart. This is acceptable because the ending is still completely satisfying, the characters having both found love in other relationships, and so it still delivers a happy ending.

When working with a writer, think carefully about the story they are trying to tell and the character at the heart of it.

If the writer doesn't have something great or important they want to say – then the script must at least be a fantastic execution of a genre. Otherwise, it offers little to satisfy.

Define the genre by answering the following:

- How would you describe the protagonist? Are they a hero? Victim? 'Everyman'?

- Is the main conflict internal or external?

- What kind of journey are they on?

- Where do they begin their journey and where do they end up?

- What actually happens? Can you define the catalytic moment – or point of no return for the protagonist – that takes place in the first act?

- How would you describe the antagonist?

- What kind of emotional experience will the audience be expecting? How are they supposed to feel by the end?

Further thoughts:

- The antagonist needs to be created with the protagonist in mind. Make sure the obstacles facing the protagonist work well with the motivations and actions of the antagonist. The more realistic the antagonist is, the more realistic the main dramatic conflict of the story will be.

- Don't let antagonists be overly simplistic or stereotypical. Make sure they are believable and have clearly defined wants and needs and that they are on a journey of their own.

- If an antagonist has no existence outside of the protagonist's story, then it will probably feel underdeveloped. Work with the writer and have them review what kind of life they are leading; what their fears are; who they love; what aspects of their character will make us care about them.

- Can you describe the main conflict of the script in a few words? If you aren't able to do so then consider the themes and the character's wants and needs. Think about what they need to learn about themselves to achieve their goal.

The script editor's job is to make sure the writer is comfortable with the conventions of the genre they are writing, and help them to use these as a guide to map out their story. And help them NOT to overcomplicate their story by picking too many genres – such as crime/thriller/horror... it's better to pick one as the primary genre and to stay with it; otherwise the writer risks missing the mark on all of them.

The most important thing to remember about genre is that these are merely conventions, not rules. They will help determine what the audience's expectations will be, and if the writer is tuned into those expectations, they have a much greater chance of satisfying them.

THE SCRIPT **REPORT**

SCRIPT REPORTS

SCRIPT COVERAGE

There are two kinds of script reports, each with a different objective in mind. The first is an evaluation of a script for a development executive, a production company or a producer. Reports for development executives and production companies, etc., are known as 'coverage' or 'script coverage' and what is required for those types of reports will vary from company to company. Most companies require concise notes that include a synopsis, direct comments as to the script's strengths and weaknesses, and the reader's overall evaluation. They usually ask whether the reader would 'pass' on it, meaning it's not worth continuing to pursue, or whether the reader thinks it is commendable and worthy of greater consideration.

Consideration can take many forms depending on what specifically the producers or production companies are looking for. Some companies cultivate writing talent and others are only interested in filling their production slate. So, greater consideration can mean various things: it may simply mean that the script will be given a second read and considered as a potential project, or it may mean that, although the script itself is not right for the company, the writer shows great promise and is someone the producers should consider for other projects. In any case, coverage reports are vitally important to the process.

A word of warning:

Coverage reports are not intended for the writers, and script editors and readers will sometimes feel free to be less sensitive in these types of reports, but I warn you against that type of thinking. I recommend that you only write what you would be comfortable with the writer seeing. I remain sensitive in all my reports, giving honest, helpful criticism in a constructive and respectful way. I believe it is wise to assume that anything I have said or written will get back to the writer, and do not want to cause unnecessary harm or discouragement by being lazy or flippant with my observations.

DEVELOPMENT REPORTS FOR A WRITER

The second kind of report is done to provide a constructive critique intended specifically for the writer on their project. Reports written for a writer about their project (which may also involve working with a development team) require a much more detailed, analytical and diagnostic assessment of the work.

This is the kind of report we will primarily be focusing on in this book.

INVESTIGATING THE SCRIPT

If you were to consult with a selection of professional script editors, you would find what is also true of writers: that each works in their own unique way. I will go into detail here as to my personal process, but this is just one way – so adapt it as you see fit.

First, I find a time when I know I will not be interrupted. It's important to me that I read the screenplay straight through as that will give me the best true sense of how the script is working overall. I shut the phone off and pretty much ignore any and all distractions in order to get a cohesive sense of the script.

As I read, I will visualise each moment of the screenplay. I'll take notes as I go, identifying my emotional reactions and notate any sections that stand out as good, bad or indifferent. I will mark page numbers down next to my notes so that I can refer back quickly.

After I have read the script through, I will then write down all of my initial reactions. How I felt about the story: the characters, the theme, how the pace was, how the dialogue worked, if there were any logic problems, any story strands that need addressing, any outstanding questions that I have. I will also write down if I was bored at any point or found it difficult to understand any portions of the story or dialogue. I will consider how the story ended, if it was satisfying or if there were too many loose ends left.

I will then write a synopsis from memory. This will help to illuminate the strongest, and possibly weakest, aspects of the script and make it easy to see which scenes, themes and characters, etc., stand out. I will also try to articulate the premise of the story in terms of the dramatic conflict by asking:

- Who is the story about?
- What do they want/need?
- Why can't they get it?

By asking questions, I will analyse the story thoroughly, making more detailed notes about how the elements of the screenplay are working, or not working. For example, if I don't empathise with a character (and I am meant to) I'll find out why. Perhaps there aren't enough scenes with that character to involve me with them; perhaps not enough information has been given telling us that character's motivation, and therefore their actions seem unclear. In this manner I figure out where the strengths and weaknesses are and seek solutions to any identified problems.

Writing the report helps me to diagnose where improvements need to be made, and how best to help the writer find ways in which they can strengthen weaker elements of the script. Once I have assessed the entire script I will write up a set of development notes.

INVESTIGATING THE SCRIPT - A CHECKLIST

- Read the script in one uninterrupted sitting. This will give you the best true sense of how the script is working overall.

- Make sure that you read everything – scene headings, action lines, as well as the dialogue. If you skip ahead you will not be able to visualise the complete story.

- Take time to visualise each moment of action in your mind.

- Take notes as you go. Write down anything that strikes you. Notate sections to review in depth later. Jot down page numbers for easy reference.

- Ignore typos, misspellings or formatting errors unless they make the story illegible. You are not proofreading the material yet – and at this stage of the process, minor mistakes are not important.

Some tips:

- Begin the report as soon as you have finished reading the script. The longer you wait, the less specific your notes will be.

- Write down what your gut reactions are. What you feel emotionally and what your initial thoughts and opinions are.

- Make notes about what expectations you had for the characters and the story – and consider how they progressed. Was it satisfying? This will help you find the central ideas and genre of the script.

- Write the synopsis from memory. This will help to illuminate the strongest, and possibly weakest, aspects of the script and make it easy to see which scenes, themes and characters, etc., stand out.

- Try to articulate the premise of the story in terms of the dramatic conflict by asking who the story is about; what they want/need; and why they can't get it.

- Review your notes. Analyse the story thoroughly. Figure out where the strengths and weaknesses are.

- Seek solutions to any identified problems.

- After you've written down your initial reactions, remember to step back and try to be objective – initial reactions are very important and extremely helpful BUT that is only part of the job. A report of value is only going to be achieved by diving deeply into the story and examining the work from all angles – and that takes time.

WRITING THE REPORT

A script report is generally between five and ten pages long, and it includes a breakdown of the story and an assessment of the script's suitability for production.

There is no set standard in the film industry for the writing of a script report, but Lucy Scher, director of the Script Factory in London, has established what I consider the best and most succinct way of organising the analytical aspects of a script report. She has also written a brilliant book that I highly recommend called *Reading Screenplays: How to Analyse and Evaluate Film Scripts*.

Every script report should include the following sections:

- Synopsis
- Premise
- Structure
- Character
- Dialogue
- Visual grammar
- Pace
- Conclusion

SYNOPSIS

There are three different types of synopses.

1. A synopsis the script reader/editor constructs for their script report in order to interpret and confirm the story concept with a writer.

2. A synopsis the writer constructs in order to clarify the structural elements of a story. Writers usually wait to write a synopsis until after the script is completed, and this is mostly for pitching purposes. However, it can also be a very useful development tool. If a writer needs assistance organising their thoughts early in the writing process, I will sometimes recommend that they start by writing one – even before they begin their first draft. (This is especially useful for less experienced writers.) A well thought through synopsis is an effective tool to help develop an idea. It's not an easy task and writers often find it hard to distil their screenplay ideas down to such a shortened form. It takes discipline, but it is immensely useful in clarifying and focusing the central ideas of a story – and it will certainly be used once they start pitching.

3. A synopsis constructed as a pitching document, written by the writer (often with help from a script editor) and used to pitch the story or script in order to gain creative interest or funding.

Synopsis included in the script report

A synopsis is simply a brief description of the screenplay, but it is an important tool. Writing the synopsis forces you to distil the story elements down, examining if it can be presented clearly in a concise and logical way – with a beginning, middle and end. If it can, then that is a good indication that the story works. If it cannot, that usually means there are problems with the construction or concept of the narrative. This process will reveal where the complications and confusions exist – and help you and the writer decipher how to proceed.

The purpose of including a synopsis in the script report is to communicate to the writer how you are interpreting the work. The reader must earn the writer's trust and that can only happen by demonstrating an understanding of the writing. Giving a synopsis will not only demonstrate that you are clear about the central idea, basic structure and themes of the work; it will also convey back to the writer how those elements are working and ensure you are in agreement.

Writing a synopsis for your writer

A typical synopsis consists of a plot summary of the screenplay that usually contains no more than three paragraphs, one for each act. The first paragraph sets up the story, the second describes what happens and the third reveals how it resolves. The synopsis should feature the main characters, what they go through during the story, their conflicts and obstacles, and the resolution.

Begin the script report synopsis by writing it in the same order as the screenplay.

Paragraph one should include the following information:

- List where and when the story is set.

- Whose story is it?

- Tell us the character's situation at the beginning of the film and what happens to disrupt their lives and change their direction.

Paragraph two should include the following information:

- Describe what the character wants and needs now that the life-changing event has happened.

- Tell us what stands in their way, making the object of their desire difficult to obtain.

- Tell us what then happens that makes it even more crucial for them to obtain it.

Paragraph three should include the following information:

- Tell us how the character achieves their goal or what ultimately stops them from achieving it.

- Tell us what has changed about the character and their situation at the end of the film.

Example of a synopsis – *A Few Good Men*

A young and inexperienced US Navy lawyer leads the defence in the court martial of two Marines, Corporal Dawson and Private Downey, accused of murdering a fellow Marine at the Guantanamo Bay Naval Base, which is under the command of Colonel Jessup. The victim, Private Santiago, compared unfavourably to his fellow Marines, had poor relations with them, and failed to respect the chain of command in attempts at being transferred. After a heated argument among the higher-ranking officers, Lieutenant Markinson advocates that Santiago be transferred immediately, but Jessup prohibits it and orders Lieutenant Kendrick, Santiago's commanding officer, to retain him and train him to become a better Marine.

When Dawson and Downey are arrested, naval investigator and lawyer Galloway suspects they carried out a 'code red' order, a violent extrajudicial punishment. Galloway requests that she be allowed to defend them, but the case is assigned to the untested Kaffee instead. Kaffee tries to plea-bargain the case, but the accused refuse to go along; they insist they were ordered by Kendrick to shave Santiago's head and did not intend for their victim to die. Kaffee, realising that he is being stretched beyond his capabilities, tries to step down as counsel. When he discovers he was assigned the case due to his poor reputation, he sees it as a challenge. Someone high up doesn't want the case to go to court and that revelation, along with some pressure from Galloway, pushes Kaffee to risk everything and decide to go to trial.

During the trial, it is established that code reds are standard at Guantanamo, as a means of getting screw-ups to straighten out. Galloway convinces Kaffee to call Jessup as a witness at great risk to his career. After questioning Jessup aggressively and comparing him to Santiago, Kaffee accuses Jessup of ordering a code red on Santiago. The prosecution and the judge object, but Jessup is caught in a lie. He stated Santiago was to be transferred off base for his safety in case other Marines sought retribution, but he also stated Marines are honourable and always follow orders. Kaffee argues that if the other Marines were ordered to leave Santiago alone, and if they do in fact always follow orders, Santiago would not have been in danger. Thus, Jessup's argument that Santiago was to be transferred was a lie. Jessup furiously explodes, accusing Kaffee of being disrespectful of a Marine doing his duty, and he admits to ordering the code red. Jessup angrily justifies his actions on the basis of national security, but is arrested and the defendants are found not guilty. However, the two Marines are dishonourably discharged for causing Santiago's death through their 'conduct unbecoming a United States Marine'. Downey is distraught, but Dawson accepts the verdict, explaining that they failed to stand up for those too weak to stand up for themselves. As the two prepare to leave, Kaffee tells Dawson he doesn't need a Marine patch on his arm to have honour. Dawson, who had previously been reluctant to respect Kaffee as an officer, now reverentially salutes him.

Keep in mind:

- The synopsis is not the place to begin your commentary; here you should be only matter of fact about the plot of the script.

- Secondary characters can be introduced, but keep it simple. Naming too many characters can make the synopsis hard to follow – again, prioritise.

- Include the most important conflict or events in the story.

- Use the present tense.

- Write synopsis paragraphs in a logical way, so they tell the story and flow together.

- Include a sentence or two about the ending scenes and how the story concludes.

- Make sure the story is clear and understandable. If the script is illogical or nonsensical, do your best to unravel it, and use that as a basis for your commentary later.

Answer the following questions:

- Does the synopsis give an accurate view of the story?
- Based on the synopsis, could you easily pitch the screenplay to others?
- Can the synopsis be easily understood? Or is it overly complicated, containing too many unnecessary details?

If the answer is NOT YES to all of the above questions, the synopsis needs more work.

PREMISE

Piloting through the language of the story development maze is one of the more frustrating issues facing screenwriters. This problem is epitomised by the interchangeable use of terms such as 'premise line', 'premise', 'logline' and 'tagline'. These terms are used in varying ways constantly, sometimes even in the same sentence. I hope that this section will help clarify any confusion you might have about them.

Distinguishing between the story's premise, a premise line and a logline

The story premise of a film or screenplay is the fundamental concept that drives the plot. It is the essence of what the script is about, the dramatic concept from which the rest of the story flows, and from which the conflict and subsequent events ensue. I've also heard it called the 'mission statement' of the film – and that's a powerful way of looking at it. Without a premise, a script would have no structure or foundation; the content would be nothing more than a series of unfocused events without a beginning, middle or end, and with no deliberate purpose or intention. A masterfully constructed story takes concentrated effort, and the premise is the heart and soul of that effort.

Industry people will often say 'the premise' this, and 'the premise' that, when they actually mean the premise line.

*The premise line is a tool used to encapsulate
and express the script's premise.*

The premise line is a succinct description that conveys the meaning and essence of the script. It should be concise, but it can be longer than one line. The premise line should include a sense of the main character, mention the event that starts the action, and give an idea of how the story concludes.

The story's premise and premise line go hand in hand. If the story's premise is not understood, then it will be impossible to compose an effective premise line.

The premise is NOT a one-line summary of the script.

To confuse things further – a premise line is regularly confused with a logline.

A logline is the story concept of a script/film in one short and snappy sentence conveying the central proposition of the film. (Again, premise lines are longer, more detailed, although still brief.)

A logline (sometimes called a tagline) provides a tempting soundbite of the story and is used to sell tickets and printed on film posters.

*Premise lines and loglines are not included in a script editor's
report BUT an account and assessment of the premise
and how it is working must be.*

Examples of premise lines and loglines

Using *The Godfather* as an example, here is how these might work:

Story premise: Michael Corleone, the innocent son of a Mafia don, resists association with his family, promising not to become involved in the family business. His resistance stops when his father is shot and all of his family's power is threatened. The feuding New York families are a great threat and Michael believes he is the only one capable of preserving the family. He changes from believing that what his family does is wrong to believing the crimes committed are a necessary evil. Michael takes no responsibility for them, but instead insists that he has no choice.

Vito Corleone is the moral centre of the film. He is old, wise and opposed to the Mafia families dealing in drugs. One of the strongest scenes in the script is the Mafia gathering at which he argues this point. When he realises he is in the minority, he is forced to acquiesce in order to bring Michael back from Italy. He promises not to interfere or seek vengeance for his other son's death – but warns them that, if anything happens to Michael, they will pay.

Michael returns home. The more he does to lead the Corleones through their difficult time, the deeper he becomes involved, and the closer he gets to obtaining the position he never thought (or admitted) he wanted – being the Godfather. He loves his wife and tries to maintain the lie that he is not a murderer. His wife represents his original desire to remain outside of his family's dirty business and live a clean life. In the end, Michael reluctantly becomes the Godfather, maintaining the belief that he is the one who will keep the Corleone family and the power structure of New York's underground soundly preserved. Michael's decision to become the new Godfather leads to the 'baptism of blood' massacre – killing all of his enemies to 'clean the family up'. He reasons it was another necessary evil. His wife starts to question how deeply he has sunk into the crime family, and his need to prevent her from knowing that part of him shows that he is still conflicted about his choices – about who he is, and what he originally wanted from life.

This script offers strong, complex, interesting and emotional relationships. It views this crime family from the inside out, offering a unique perspective. The real world is replaced by an authoritarian patriarchy where power and justice flow from the Godfather, and the only villains are those who are traitors to the family.

Premise line: When the innocent, youngest son of a powerful Mafia don discovers his beloved father has been shot as part of a territory war, he agrees to join the family to get revenge and re-establish the family's honour, until his actions force him to cross a line he never intended to cross, dooming him to become the next Godfather.

Logline: The youngest son of a Mafia don takes revenge on the men who shot his father and becomes the new Godfather.

Using *E.T. The Extra-Terrestrial* as an example, here is how these might work:

Premise line: A troubled child summons the courage to help a friendly alien escape Earth and return to his home planet.

Logline (from one of the early posters): He is afraid. He is totally alone. He is 3 million light years from home.

Using *Alien* as an example, here is how these might work:

Premise line: The commercial vessel *Nostromo* receives a distress call from an unexplored planet. After searching for survivors, the crew heads home only to realise that a deadly bioform has joined them.

Logline (from one of the early posters): In space, no one can hear you scream.

Using *A Few Good Men* as an example, here is how these might work:

Premise line: When a plea-bargaining Navy lawyer takes on a case against the commanding officer who ordered the hazing of the screw-up Marine his clients are accused of murdering, he risks his career.

Logline (from one of the early posters): In the heart of the nation's capital, in a courthouse of the US government, one man will stop at nothing to keep his honour, and one will stop at nothing to find the truth.

Hopefully these examples clearly illustrate the difference between these tools: the story premise is the mission statement; the premise line is the succinct, two-line encapsulation of the story's heart; and a logline is a soundbite used to attract an audience.

Premise in a script report

Hopefully the difference between the story's premise and a premise line is now clear. This is significant because the script report is constructed from the analysis of the script's premise, and will greatly determine whether the story is strong enough to make a good film (or television show).

Finding the premise requires an in-depth examination of the script and consolidation of the elements found within.

The premise always answers two key questions:

What is the story AND what is the story about?

- *What is the story?* This refers to dramatic conflict. What does the main character have to overcome or achieve in the story?

- *What is the story about?* This refers to thematic conflict. What ideas, truths or life issues are being explored in the story? What does the resolution of the story suggest?

The answers to these questions form the premise of the story. So, to find the story premise, the script editor must again:

- Look at what the ideas, truths and issues explored in the story are.

- Look at the main character and understand what their goal, want or need is.

- Look at what is standing in their way of achieving it.

Conflict

When considering these elements in the script, it helps to understand how conflict works.

Conflict unfolds in three different ways in film:

- *Interpersonal conflicts – man versus man.* The character's problem stems chiefly from other characters (parents disallowing certain activities, like the dancing restriction in *Footloose*, or being the victim of a stalker).

- *Situational/environmental – man versus nature.* The character's problem stems from the outside world that they inhabit (uncontrollable circumstances such as a natural crisis like a tsunami, or an illness).

- *Internal – man versus self.* The character's problem stems from their personality and worsens because of it.

Ideally all three types of conflict are woven into the story, but that can take time. It is better to have the writer focus on one main conflict initially and then weave the others in during later drafts.

Again using *The Godfather* as an example, the initial conflict facing the main character, Michael, is the shooting of his father (situational/external – man versus man).

His desire for revenge pulls him into the dangerous world of the Mafia (internal – man versus self).

The power and politics of his new position make it impossible for him to walk away once he has joined the mob (interpersonal – man versus nature).

An argument is not the same as dramatic conflict, at least not the deep-rooted type of conflict that will drive a screenplay. In the real world, arguments are, for the most part, trivial and uninteresting to everyone except those involved. True dramatic conflict stems from a much deeper source, and is rooted in the subtext of the central characters, driven by their fundamentally conflicting desires, and is revealed by exploring their opposing ideas.

Some sure-fire killers of dramatic conflict are:

- Characters speaking all their subtext. Spoken subtext drains the conflict between characters and inhibits character development. That's how you can end up with just an argument instead of real dramatic conflict.

- Characters agreeing about everything. Characters need to have opposing ideas to be interesting. If they're too warm and cosy, we won't be interested.

- Characters turning the other cheek. In real life, that's a great way to avoid conflict, but screenplays NEED conflict. So, turning the other cheek is exactly the opposite of what needs to happen in a script.

Keep in mind:

- The premise in your report must communicate the essence of the story and convey three main pieces of information:

  i. What the main conflict of the story is
  ii. What the dramatic strength of the story is
  iii. What the thematic strength of the story idea is

- There needs to be enough conflict to sustain an audience's interest. Remember that, without conflict, there is no story. There has to be enough at stake to make the audience care how the story resolves.

- The conflict of the story needs to be situated right and progress effectively. Presenting it either too early or too late can pose problems.

- The conflict needs to remain consistent. If the conflict changes within the story too drastically, the film will seem unfocused and most likely be unsatisfying.

- The protagonist must be the character living out the conflict. If the story revolves around a character who is not experiencing the conflict, it will not have significant impact.

- Themes emerge from story conflicts/tension, and the meaning of the film is a result of the resolution of the conflict.

  Writers write in order to express their views – their films have a viewpoint on their subject matter and it is within that viewpoint that the story has resonance.

Things to include in your report:

- State what you consider the themes or potential themes of the script to be.

- If possible, articulate what the story is saying about the themes it is exploring.

- Consider whether the themes explored are likely to interest an audience.

- Mention if there are areas that conflict or confuse the theme or meaning of the script.

- State whether the events in the story are conveyed well, or whether they are heavy-handed or confused.

- Discuss how the theme works within its chosen genre.

Remember: investigating the story premise of the script is an essential part of the process; the information gathered here will provide the foundation for the rest of your notes.

STRUCTURE

For the purposes of the script report, it is essential that the script editor assesses how well the writer has organised the story and the protagonist's journey within it.

Consider these questions on structure when you write your report:

The set-up

- Does the story begin at the correct moment in time? (Or does it start too early so that nothing happens for too long? Or begin too late so that too much explanation is needed about past events?)

- Is the main character introduced clearly and quickly?

- Is the main conflict introduced clearly and quickly?

- Is the world or the character clear so we can engage with them?

- Is the antagonist clearly identified?

- Is the genre clear?

- Has the writer set the tone early on? (Is it clear what kind of film this is?)

The story

- Is there a clear beginning, middle and end?

- Is there a clear moment (inciting incident) in the early part of the story that gets the story started?

- Is the story consistent and does it explore the dramatic question throughout?

- Is there a strong midpoint that propels the story forward?

- Is there a logical progression of events?

- Do the subplots work with the main story?

- Is there enough conflict within the story?

- Is the story understandable or is it complex and too confusing?

- Is the writing choosing the best moments to show the audience, or is too much of the dramatic content being dealt with off screen?

- Is the story told in the most compelling way?

CHARACTER

Characters are the people who inhabit a story, and what makes a character memorable is expressed in its very definition. The word character literally means the mental and moral qualities distinctive to an individual. The quality of their personality, their nature, disposition, temperament, mentality, temper, psychology, psyche – their overall make-up. It's the essence of who they are – and that is what a writer needs to establish in order to create a convincing and memorable character.

Without characters there is no story; they dictate which direction a story will take and so, from that point of view, all films are character-driven, even those that seem plot-driven.

A writer defines these qualities as they craft each of their characters by inventing their backstories (their history) and motivations in order to create a full, rich and believable persona. For that reason, having a passive main character can be very problematic in a script. Of course there are exceptions, but if the main character is not capable of driving the action forward, the dramatic question becomes primarily about the character's inactivity and that can prove very limiting.

> 'When we look at films, we usually see only the action.
> Yet it is the decision to act that helps us understand
> how the character's mind works.' – Linda Seger

We know that: character + want/need + obstacles = story. Therefore it makes sense that, if a character is overly passive, and does not want or need anything, it will be harder to construct an engaging story around them.

Ending

- Does the story build to a climax that answers the dramatic question?

- Is it clear what the characters have learned at the end of the story?

- Do the scenes that follow the climax give us sufficient time to absorb what has happened without dragging the story out too much?

- Does the writing match the intended genre?

Character arc

Character arc refers to the journey of a character as they evolve throughout a narrative. A character begins the story with certain viewpoints and behaviours that change as a result of events in the story. The character arc is the status of the change they undergo as they adapt to events and challenges throughout the storyline.

Often character arcs revolve around the main character being unable to resolve their problems because they lack the skills or have a flaw that holds them back. This inability or flaw is a driving element of the story's plot. In order to improve their situation, they have to learn new skills and must gain a greater sense of self-awareness and capability. They must achieve that awareness through their relationships and environment and they will often have mentors or co-protagonists to help. Their new awareness ultimately changes who they are – or are becoming.

The character's journey

Characters have different kinds of journeys: internal, external and variations in-between, but there are generally three reasons for a character's problems:

- The character wants something, but something inside of them stops them from getting it.

- The character wants something, but something outside of themself (environmental or societal forces) prevents them from getting it.

- The character wants something, but the antagonist (enemy) doesn't want them to have it and tries to stop them.

The character section of the script report is used to examine the journey that the character is taking in the story. It is essential that the character's decisions and actions result in some kind of meaningful change at the end of the story (unless the point of the story is that they don't or can't change for some reason, and then the script must reveal their journey in that context).

Questions to ask when considering character:

- Is the character engaging and sympathetic?

- What is the character's situation?

- What are the character's actions?

- What is the character's attitude?

- Are the obstacles that the character faces intriguing?

- Can I form a picture of the character in my head?

- Do I want them to succeed?

- Do they inspire emotions in me?

- Did I enjoy spending time with them?

- Has there been enough at stake for them in the story?

- Do they externalise their inner conflict in ways that the audience can see and understand?

- Is their journey plausible?

- Are the protagonist and antagonist well matched?

- Do the characters justify their positions by fulfilling their intended dramatic or thematic function?

- Are there enough characters to fulfil the story? Too many?

- Are the characters clearly introduced so that we can engage with them?

- Are the characters well rounded? Is their behaviour plausible within the conventions of the genre?

DIALOGUE

This refers to all the words spoken by the characters. It is difficult to get right and should ideally advance the plot and reveal character.

Consider the following when reviewing dialogue:

- Remember, films are a visual medium and what can be shown should be – the writer should provide visual storytelling as well as dialogue. Look for the correct balance in each script – is there too much, or too little, dialogue?

- Does the dialogue in the script help the reader understand the characters?

- Does the dialogue support the expectations of the characters in the story and help us bond with them?

- Do we learn what we need to know through the dialogue?

- Are we being told things we do not need to know through the dialogue? If so, this needs to be expressed and substantiated in the script report.

- Remember, we also learn through what is not being said and through the sound effects and the music of a film. The silences are equally important.

- Note down any examples that you feel show strong or weak dialogue in the script.

- Always use specific examples when commenting on dialogue.

- Do the characters have unique and individual voices?

- If the character names weren't listed, could you make out which one was speaking? (Some of the time? All of the time? None of the time?)

- Are the character voices consistent?

VISUAL GRAMMAR

Visual grammar refers to the ways in which a writer uses visual elements to express their ideas and tell their story. It is important that these visual methods are brought up in the script report as they demonstrate how the writer is telling the story cinematically. Too often writers fail to consider enough of the visual elements of a script and neglect to set up the world of their screenplays.

Writing visually does not mean including camera angles in the script or telling the director how to direct the film on the page. It can allow for expressing how the film transitions from one scene into another, by using fade to, or cut to, etc., but even those explanations should be kept to a minimum.

What is essential is that the scriptwriter uses a variety of visual methods to tell the story. There are two areas of visual grammar for the writer to explore and both have equal value.

Technical tools and techniques

- Montage – a montage is a technique in film comprising a short series of shots edited into a sequence and delivering important information and time passage in a visual and economical way.

- Parallel time – is a technique whereby cutting occurs between two or more related actions occurring at the same time, in two separate locations or different points.

- Flashbacks – show memories of an earlier event or scene. The argument against using flashbacks is that they can stall the forward motion of the story, pull the audience out of the world of the film or feel like bad exposition. However, when used effectively, flashbacks can be very powerful. They tend to be used to illuminate a character's subjective understanding of their past, or show puzzling memories and often enable the audience to know the truth of what has taken place. Films like *The Godfather Part Two*, *The Sixth Sense* and *Gone Girl* use flashbacks very successfully.

- Voiceover – the use of voiceover as a commentator allows the audience to hear the private thoughts of a character or narrator in a story. It is important the voiceover adds new insight into the narrative and does not simply repeat action shown within the scene.

- Special effects – tend to be used in specific genre films, but this is becoming less true as technology continues to advance. The important thing to consider is whether the special effects described in the script feel integral to the story, make the world clear and remain consistent.

Spatial awareness

- Choice of location or locations

- Thematic imagery

- Use of day, night and weather

- Use of colour schemes and themes

- The descriptive power of scene directions – conveying as much as possible through the setting of each of the scenes

As you review the screenplay, consider each of these visual elements and discuss how the writer has incorporated them into their script.

Questions to consider regarding visual grammar:

- Does the writer understand and use visual elements in the script?

- Are these techniques being used effectively?

- Is the visual grammar of the script helping the reader to understand the world and to see it clearly?

- Does their use of visual elements contribute to the understanding of the story?

- Does the script contain enough of these techniques? Or too many?

PACE

Each scene and sequence in a script should have an appropriate rhythm and this section of the script report deals with how the writer constructs and modulates the rhythm, tempo and mood within the overall script. Writers must vary scene tempos and lengths to add tension, comedy and drama. Analysing the pace of the script will help writers understand where the story lags and where important events go by too abruptly.

Writers should enter scenes as late as possible and leave them as early as possible to avoid overwriting.

Tools used to manipulate pace are:

Compressed time

Audiences are smart and well educated in the language of film – they understand the shorthand used and do not need to be shown unnecessary, often mundane, activities in order to follow the action that is taking place.

For example, if a character is looking out of the window as a car pulls up, we don't necessarily need to see that character putting on their coat, closing and locking the door, walking to the car and then getting into the car to join their friend. We can have a compressed version of the action that 'jumps ahead', taking them straight from the window to jumping into the car. The audience will fill in the gaps if it is a logical leap forward.

In this way, writers must be economical with their writing and not overwrite or overstate the obvious. This is another area that a script editor should focus on in their report. Are the scenes written in the most effective and economical way?

Slow motion

Slow motion is a tool used to slow down the action and emphasise a moment in the script. Slowing the moment down gives the audience extra time to view the action and adds additional impact. (For example, a flying arrow may be slowed down to emphasise someone being killed, or a car accident might be done in slow motion to intensify the impact.)

Real time

Real time is when the amount of time it takes for events to happen on screen is the same as in real life. The audience sees the action take place in real time. This tool is used to emotionally engage the audience in the situation. Using real time can heighten the intensity of a scene or situation, enabling the audience to experience the event in a very immediate way.

Things to consider regarding pace:

- Do the key scenes start and end at the correct moment?
- Is the script a page-turner or does it drag in spots?
- Do the scenes vary in length and mood so as to avoid a monotonous rhythm and engage the audience effectively?
- Do the sequences build to create tension or humour as required?
- Are lengthy dialogue scenes or monologues slowing down the pace?
- Are the scene lengths suitable for the intended genre?
- Remember that the overall impact you get from the first read will give you a first impression of the story. But that is just part of the job. It is necessary to review in detail the individual scenes and sequences in order to assess how the overall pace of the script is working.

CONCLUSION

At the end of the script report it is important to include detailed comments reiterating the strengths and weaknesses of the technical and creative execution of the screenplay.

It is also important that the notes direct the writer in terms of how to proceed with their next draft, helping them prioritise and focus on how to improve the script without overwhelming them.

In addition, consideration should be given to what kind of market the film might have and helping the writer put their work into context:

- What is the potential for the script?

- Who will want to see the film? What type of audience?

- Has this kind of film been done before? What other film is it like?

- What are the most important elements the writer needs to address in their next draft?

- Remember to be honest in your comments, but also be kind. If there are serious problems in the script it is essential that you express that – but do so in a constructive, focused and thoughtful way.

Always substantiate your notes with examples, demonstrating clearly what is being said. Remember you are there to be on the writer's side and get them ready for the next draft.

A SAMPLE SCRIPT REPORT

Here is a sample of a full script report. I hope this will demonstrate clearly how a report functions to help the writer understand how the script is coming across to readers – and how to use that information to improve the work.

MOON
screenplay by Nathan Parker, story by Duncan Jones

Synopsis:

In 2035, Lunar Industries have made a fortune after an oil crisis on Earth has forced scientists to build an automated lunar facility that mines an alternative fuel, helium-3. Sam Bell, the astronaut who maintains operations on the lunar facility, nears the end of a three-year work contract as the facility's sole resident. Sam oversees automated harvesters and launches canisters bound for Earth, containing the extracted helium-3. Chronic communication problems have disabled his live feed from Earth and limit him to occasional recorded messages to his wife, Tess, who was pregnant with their daughter, Eve, when he left. His only companion is an artificial intelligence named GERTY, who assists with the base's automation and attends to Sam's day-to-day needs.

Two weeks before Sam is due to return to Earth, he begins suffering from hallucinations. One distracts him on the job causing him to crash his lunar rover into the harvester. Sam is injured and awakes in the base infirmary with no memory of the accident. He overhears GERTY receiving instructions from Lunar Industries to prevent him leaving the base and to wait for the arrival of a rescue team. Sam's suspicions aroused, he manufactures a fake problem to convince GERTY to let him outside. He travels to the crashed rover, where he finds his unconscious doppelganger. Sam brings the double back to the base and tends to his injuries. There, the two Sams start to wonder if one is a clone of the other. After a heated argument, they join forces and coerce GERTY into revealing that they are both clones of the original Sam Bell. The two Sams discover that communications are deliberately being jammed at the outermost perimeter of the base. They also learn that previous Sam clones have been euthanised and incinerated instead of being sent home as promised. Searching the facility, they uncover a secret vault containing hundreds of hibernating clones that Lunar Industries manufactures to avoid paying for new astronauts. Desperate, the elder Sam drives past the interference and calls Earth. Instead of reaching his wife, his daughter, now 15 years old, answers and tells him that Tess died 'some years ago'. When Sam hears her father, the original Sam Bell, speaking in the background, he hangs up feeling devastated.

The two Sams realise that the 'rescue' team will kill them when they arrive. The younger Sam suggests sending the other to Earth in one of the helium-3 transports, but the older Sam, knowing he is already badly deteriorated, insists the younger Sam go instead. The younger Sam agrees, and promises, when back on Earth, to alert the public to Lunar Industries' unethical practices. The older Sam plans to die by the crashed rover so Lunar Industries and the rescue team will not suspect anything until it's too late. The younger Sam orders GERTY to revive another clone to greet the rescuers, and then programmes a harvester to crash and wreck a jamming antenna, thereby enabling live communications with Earth. GERTY advises the younger Sam to reboot him, erasing any record of the event, and Sam does so. The older Sam lies back in the crippled rover and remains conscious long enough to watch the launch of the transport carrying the younger Sam to Earth. As the helium transport enters the Earth's atmosphere, news broadcasts show Sam reporting Lunar Industries, instigating a criminal prosecution against the corporation for its unethical practices. A government official retaliates by claiming that Sam is either crazy or an illegal immigrant, and should not be taken seriously. The fate of the future Sams remains undetermined.

Premise:

Just before his scheduled return home, Sam Bell, the solo astronaut in charge of maintaining operations at a lunar facility used to transport alternative fuel to Earth, becomes unwell and starts to have hallucinations. Desperate to contact his family, he is told that communications are down due to technical difficulties, and his disposition and condition only worsen. Under the stress he has an accident, and when he awakens he can't remember what has taken place and becomes utterly confused when he meets his doppelganger. He and his double quickly realise that their lives and realities have been manipulated. Sam is devastated to discover that he is one of many clones harvested by Lunar Industries to be used as free labourers, and that he is scheduled to be inhumanely destroyed – as were the two Sams who have already been euthanised and incinerated. With only days until his scheduled demise, Sam makes it his mission to save the other clones from the same awful destiny and to report the truth to the world.

There are powerful themes presented in this story. This script immediately creates dramatic tension as we witness Sam's desperate isolation, loneliness and inability to communicate with his home. It very effectively increases that tension when Sam discovers he is a clone and is to be destroyed.

Thematically this story is about human beings playing God. It explores two moral questions. First, are clones the same as real people and do they have feelings? And secondly, what responsibility does mankind have to the beings they have created? In the world of the script, clones are treated as machines (or slaves) and not as humans, but Sam behaves with more humanity than any of the human characters. In doing so, he attests that all living creatures deserve the right to be free.

Ultimately the script answers both questions it sets up, and as Sam decides to sacrifice himself and forsake his dream of returning to Earth, he ensures a better future for the next generation of clones. He proves that not only are clones feeling, human beings, but that it is his humanity that has allowed him to shoulder the responsibility of restoring the natural and correct order of things.

In other words, mankind is responsible to and for one another – a theme that has strong contemporary relevance.

Structure:

Moon unfolds in an entertaining and often surprising way.

A voiceover is used at the beginning of the script and sets up Sam's isolation in a very effective way. As Sam records a message to his wife he expresses his feelings, and through this the audience is introduced to the base and Sam's routine. By the time Sam is finished with his message we have a strong sense of the world of the script. This voiceover element is not applied again, but because it was used in the form of a message it is part of the story and using it does not feel false or unbalanced.

Setting up Sam's isolation and loneliness at the beginning of the story was a powerful choice. It immediately supplies Sam with strong human feelings and emotions and creates sympathy for him. It also makes him instantly relatable, so when the twist comes, it is a genuine surprise.

Although it was somewhat difficult to follow having two Sam characters, the script was organised well, and the concepts and events, for the most part, were clear. The one element that remained a bit confusing was Sam's intermittent visions of the little girl. The visions seemed to be there to demonstrate Sam's mental and physical breakdown and because they disappear as soon as Sam accepts the fact that he is a clone, it seems they are also there to humanise him. However, as they simply fade and are never referred to again, the thread of that story element feels incomplete and unsatisfying. I suggest this story element would benefit from being revisited and thought through in greater detail and with an eye to clarity. In all other aspects, this is a very well-constructed script.

Sleep and dreams were used effectively to monitor Sam's state of mind and to illustrate the world he is missing. In his dreams his emotions come to life and that is another way that his humanity is expressed.

The story elements in this script are woven together nicely and the climax is both moving and satisfying. In Sam's final dream, he is with his wife and, as he dies, there is a sense that he has finally got what he wanted all along. He is home.

Character:

Sam is established as a good and decent man, and because he wants nothing more than to go home to be with his family, he is quite a sympathetic character. As he shows signs of becoming ill our concern increases, and it is a surprising and crushing blow when he discovers that he is a clone and will be incinerated. His need to understand his place in the world is absolutely believable, and the fact that he sacrifices himself with courage and determination make him a heroic character.

Sam having a bit of a temper gave him additional depth that served the script in several ways. It showed that he had strength and made it believable that under pressure he would fight the system. It also showed that he had remorse when he explained to GERTY that he was sorry for showing that side of himself to his wife. His having remorse was an additional proof of his human qualities.

GERTY's character provides an additional surprise. He starts out as a programmed robot with no apparent human qualities and transitions into a pivotal resource who helps Sam. His transformation can only be explained by applying human qualities such as understanding and compassion. In this way, he is used well to support the script's theme that machines and clones have more humanity than the humans who have created them.

In *Moon* we don't get to know the bad guys personally. They have names and faces, but they are more a force of nature than actual characters. They represent the system that has created Sam's world. They are godlike in their control of him, but have no compassion or humanity. They use, manipulate and eventually destroy him. They also underestimate him and, because they do, he is able to overthrow their control.

Dialogue:

I truly enjoyed the dialogue and language of this script, which is handled in a masterful way. It's vivid, descriptive, moving and strong – and the moments of silence were also powerful.

It was essential that both the Sam characters had similar and yet unique voices. That task was fully accomplished. Older Sam has a very distinct manner and his being tired and drained gave him an edgier and wearier tone, while the younger Sam sounded cooler and generally more relaxed. The result was very effective.

GERTY's dialogue is clearly that of a robot, but even so, a unique personality comes through. He develops nicely as the script progresses and becomes more human when he eventually helps Sam. Nevertheless, his robot-like manner is sustained, keeping his personality completely consistent while offering up very interesting additional dimensions to him.

It is also worth noting that there are a substantial number of scenes that contain little or no dialogue in this script, but they too function very well. Because the descriptive action, storyline and atmosphere are well crafted and significant tension and emotion are sustained throughout, the story remains interesting and consistently strong.

I particularly responded to the moment just after Sam has spoken to his daughter; when he hears the original Sam Bell's voice, he hangs up feeling completely shattered. We see him from outside the rover in the vast landscape of space and, in the 'unrelenting' moon silence, he sobs. That sob was very powerful and completely supported the tone and dynamic nature of the script.

Pace:

The pace in this script is strong and moves along very well while delivering lots of intriguing plot twists and turns. The scene lengths vary a great deal, which helps to keep the energy up and move the story along effectively. Many of the scenes have little or no dialogue and are primarily visual, but the descriptions are written concisely without being distracting or slowing the story down.

There is a ticking-clock element that begins when the rescue unit is sent to the base, and this helps to strongly increase the urgency in the last act.

Visual grammar:

This script creates a very complete and believable world and is atmospheric throughout.

The early scenes establish the relationship between the base, the Moon and Earth and provide a strong sense of isolation and alienation. There is a vast difference between the enormous space outside the base and claustrophobic space inside the facility, and that relationship amplifies Sam's loneliness and vulnerability. The miniature town Sam is carving as a hobby throughout the script is a powerful visual device expressing his desperate need for companionship and civilisation.

Despite what could be a confusing concept to read (the many versions of Sam), the visual clues are placed well, enabling the story to be easily understood. For instance, providing older Sam with facial hair, a messy and more aged look, along with a burnt hand, were simple and realistic ways of differentiating him from the younger version, who is clean-shaven, neater and uninjured. These descriptions made it possible to follow the story with little confusion, and it will certainly be even easier to follow once on film.

One extraordinary image is in the scene where the two Sams discover the room of sleeping clone pods. That image escalates the urgency of their situation and gives the older Sam potent motivation to face his situation. In that instant he knows that he can no longer deny the truth of his situation.

Conclusion:

Moon was a very enjoyable read. The characters are likable and the story is told in an entertaining and engaging way. The themes are powerful and convey poignant moral messages without being preachy. The bittersweet ending is very satisfying and heartfelt. This is a commendable script, indeed, and one that is very marketable. Not only is it a strong, well-crafted story, but it is entertaining and suspenseful and a good match for anyone who enjoys fantasy/ science fiction, or just a good, compelling drama.

THINGS TO REMEMBER WHEN WRITING YOUR REPORT

- Prioritise your comments – and be aware of not overloading the writer. If you have two important notes and one less significant one, consider waiting to give the lesser note. It is best to focus on the important notes first. Chances are there will be a rewrite in which the minor note might no longer be an issue.

- Always present the material in its best possible light. Consider not only the script, but also the story material. What is working/ what isn't? Highlight the potential – this will really help open up communication later.

- Make a point of highlighting aspects of the script that work well. The writer needs a balanced critique and it's important to emphasise the things that are working. The writer is likely to be more receptive to criticism if they have also been given praise where it is due.

- Maintain an objective tone. Stick to third person and avoid using 'I'. Using 'the audience' is fine, and you can refer to the writer as 'the writer' if needed.

- Be accurate. Make sure you have all the facts right and that you have spelt the characters' names and locations, etc., correctly.

- Write your report in the present tense. Writing in the present tense keeps the energy of the report active. Do not use the past tense in the synopsis unless you are referring to a section from the past, revealed through flashbacks or dialogue.

- Make sure your comments are specific. Generalisations are not helpful to a writer and will only cause frustration. Substantiate all of your points with specific examples.

- Make sure your report is written intelligibly and well thought through – present your ideas in an organised, clear and logical way.

- Typos and mistakes will undermine your credibility. Make sure to spell characters' names and story elements correctly – don't be sloppy with the details.

- Reference to other films can be useful in clarifying points, but make sure that your references are accurate and familiar. It will not help the writer if the film reference is unknown to them or if the reference is unclear or has no bearing on the issue raised.

- If the script is very similar to another film or script you have seen, it is important that you let the writer know. Again, be gentle with this.

- Do not offer specific fixes to any of the problems you expose in the script. Instead ask appropriate questions that will guide the writer towards finding their own answers and solutions.

- Be as encouraging and supportive as possible. Writing is a sensitive process. You have been hired to assist the writer – that is your number-one duty. Do so with patience and integrity.

THE FIRST **MEETING**

Where in the process the writer is with their script will determine the agenda of your first meeting. But wherever that is – the important thing is to be prepared! Know as much as you can about the writer and their work. Give yourself time to read through all materials provided, and to digest and assemble what your reactions are to the work without feeling rushed. Have good, clear notes ready to refer to. This is especially important during the earlier part of your career. It takes time to create a process of working, and giving yourself ample time to prepare and do the groundwork will allow you to be relaxed and focused when you meet with writers.

The worst thing a development person can do is be inaccurate about the material, and by that I am not referring to having a difference of opinion, but making factual errors. Don't use the wrong name when referring to a character – that type of thing. Nothing disappoints a writer like being misunderstood, or having their work disregarded, and that is certainly not the way in which you want to start a working relationship. In fact, that will put an end to one very quickly. So, go in prepared.

Often, you will have already done a script report and, in that case, much of your discussion will be focused on those notes and helping the writer clarify any concerns or remaining questions. Make sure to review your report/notes prior to the meeting and have the material fresh in your mind.

The first meeting will last approximately 90 minutes. The writer should leave with a plan for how to move forward with the script, and a strategy for how the script editor and they will work together and organise a work schedule – if that is desired.

DEADLINES AND SCHEDULING

Some writers prefer not to have a fixed schedule and, again, that is something that needs to be decided depending on the individual circumstances. If there is nothing pressing, no approaching deadlines, then begin by working in the manner the writer prefers – this may simply be to set up the next meeting or a small goal. Adopt the pace that suits the writer – but be aware that, ultimately, writers will need to meet deadlines and getting into the practice will help in the long run. Whenever possible, I do set up goals and deadlines because often not doing so leads to slow progress and too much procrastination. If, over time, you discover that to be true for one of your writers, readdress the issue with them. Gently explain that, if they truly wish to progress, creating a schedule will help.

PREPARING FOR THE MEETING

The developer's job is to help the writer tell their story as well as they possibly can and during this meeting the goal is to help sort out the priorities for the next draft by discussing the sources of the weaknesses in the script and the potential ways forward.

Prior to the first meeting read the script and prepare some feedback/a report on the current draft and/or documents you were given. The first meeting will generally cover the writer's intentions for the script, their plans for the next draft and their aspirations for the project within the film industry.

The writer needs to know you are clear about the story THEY are trying to tell. One way to ensure that you are on the same wavelength is to give them a copy of your synopsis. This will open up a dialogue – and you will quickly know if you are on the correct track or not.

- Arrange for the meeting to be held in a calm environment where there will be as few distractions as possible. Try to avoid having food involved, as that will dissipate the focus of the discussion.

- Know the material well, so that you won't have to flip through the script. Have notes that you refer to.

- Don't go for longer than two hours. It's difficult to maintain concentration for longer, and will start to bring diminishing returns.

THINGS TO DISCUSS

Make sure that you are clear about the genre and story tone the writer is going for. This is especially important if it is commission work or intended for a specific market. I've seen writers become terribly frustrated because they have been writing a draft with a specific tone or concept in mind, only to discover that their producers or commissioners have very different ideas of what they want. This can be avoided by having clear and open discussions of what is intended and expected up front.

Prioritise your notes. There is no point in spending tons of time discussing minute details if there are significant structural or story problems. For example, if the answers to certain big questions are not clear from the script – such as whose story this is, and what the story question and genre are – then those issues need to be addressed first. There is little benefit to be had from mentioning that the formatting isn't correct, or that there are typos or small inconsistencies. Use your best judgement – and help the writer create order.

Giving too many notes all at once, especially when there are bigger issues at hand, can be very counterproductive. Be aware that writers don't always know what is best for them during the process, especially new writers who are just developing. If given the choice, most writers will be eager to hear ALL of your notes at once. This is not always advisable. Use your best judgement. You don't want to waste precious time or slow the writer down, but you do not want to overwhelm them either. So, if you are in the early stages of development, and if it doesn't feel essential – save the note for another day. Keep in mind that, frequently, once the major issues within a script have been addressed, smaller notes often get worked out naturally, even without you having to mention them.

THE WRITER'S PROCESS – AND KEEPING A LOG

It helps to understand what a writer's process is. The first meeting is a good time to spend a few minutes breaking the ice, getting to know where they write, what time of day they write, when they take breaks, how they want to be reached, and how they want to receive their notes. Some writers prefer not to be given written notes and would rather have discussions about the work. If this is the case, you must still make your own set of notes to work from – and I highly recommend that after your discussion you follow up with an email or memo recording what has been discussed and decided, along with how you and the writer have agreed to proceed. This doesn't have to be overly formal, but it's important to keep records of the progression, particularly if you are working on behalf of a production. It's always wise to keep a log of the work. You never know when you will need to refer back to a conversation you had months ago about a specific draft, and the notes you keep will be the only record you have of what has transpired during the development process.

Also, over the years you will hopefully work with many writers. If you keep records of your progress, those notes will help remind you in the future of how best to assist the writer – and what their work patterns and preferences are. These may change to a degree as time passes, so do check in again with them and make sure to keep up-to-date notes.

THINGS TO REMEMBER

Some of these notes may seem obvious, but I am listing them anyway:

- Be on time – or early. It starts the meeting off on the wrong foot if you are late. (If they are late, let it go – but if it happens again make them aware that your time is valuable and must be respected.)

- Make sure that you have means to contact one another in case something unforeseen happens, someone gets lost or delayed or there is an unexpected change of plan.

- Start the meeting on a positive note. This will get things moving in the right direction for both of you. If you can't think of anything positive to say about the script, then simply acknowledge the hard work that went into it. It's not easy to write a script – even a bad one.

- Most first scripts are terrible. Most first drafts are terrible. Don't judge too harshly – this is a process! Just focus on helping make the next draft better.

- Sometimes writers take notes very personally. If this happens, try to remind the writer that your comments are about the story and are NOT personal.

- Experienced writers tend to take script notes much easier than newer writers – but that is not always the case. Give your notes respectfully and remember storytelling is subjective; your notes are your opinion, hopefully a well thought through and educated opinion, but even so, there are many ways of telling a story. Stand by your views, substantiate your notes, but keep an open mind – and proceed gently. An upset writer isn't going to hear your points anyway, but an encouraged one will. So, think about how you communicate your concerns.

- Use questions to express your concerns. For example, if a script has logic problems, ask the writer to simply tell you the story. As they do, and as the areas of concern come up, ask the writer to explain what has happened there. Let them know that there is information missing or something that is unclear. By asking questions that reveal where the problems are, they will hopefully see where things need improvement.

- Don't give specific plot suggestions. This is not your script and your job is to help writers find their own answers. Ask questions of the material rather than dictating ideas.

As relationships develop writers will ask you for your specific ideas when they are stuck. The best way to handle those requests is by discussing their issues and, in turn, asking them questions that guide them to their own answers. However, sometimes the writer will be truly despairing and you may feel that you need to offer them a lifeline in the form of an idea... you must make a judgement call – but I warn you not to make a habit of this. Why? **Because, it is not your script. Your job is to help writers find their own answers.** Offering up specific solutions may not really help. Your suggestion might solve one problem, but end up causing others down the line. Think of it like this – have you ever watched a wildlife show and seen a creature going through a difficult time, maybe even starving? The crews are never allowed to interfere with the animals' natural habitat and so should not feed them, or 'fix' things for them. They want to help, but if they do it might seriously disrupt the natural course of things. This is the same principle... yes, you might want to offer solutions, but it's better to help them find their own solutions.

But, I would be lying if I didn't admit that I have on occasion offered up a suggestion when it was specifically asked for, and when I felt it might really help. (Yes, I am the kind of person who wouldn't be able to let the animal starve and would have to sneak them something if I felt it was the right thing to do.) So, if a writer asks me directly for this kind of help, I will seldom do it – but I have... it's hard not to, especially when a writer is on a deadline and really struggling and you have a perfectly good idea that seems like it will help. Even then, I will do what I can to try and help the writer come to that conclusion without spelling it out, or giving too much detail. And if I do offer up this kind of help, I also warn them that it might not work entirely and that they need to really think it through and make sure it works with their plan for the film. I am more likely to do this with newer writers who are exploring possibilities in their work and script. I will try to approach it as an exercise and NOT offer it up as a fixed resolution.

- Take notes at the meeting. Make sure you keep a log of what you have discussed and how things are going to proceed. Make sure the writer is also taking down any necessary notes. Have an extra pen and paper available – in case they forgot to bring one.

- After the meeting, send the writer a document detailing what has been discussed and decided, along with reminders of what to do next.

- Do not set up unrealistic deadlines. Better to set up reasonable deadlines and progress steadily.

- Before you end the meeting set up your next point of contact. Put a date in the diary for your next meeting. It's always better to work face to face, but sometimes that is not possible. If you are working with a writer who is a long distance away, Skype is a very useful tool. It's free and it allows you to work directly even from a distance.

- Keep records of the process. Note down all that has been discussed and keep a log of your meetings and correspondence. It's important to keep accurate records.

- If for any reason the meeting is going badly, end it early. Give the writer and yourself time to reassess what was not working and reschedule.

- Never lie or fabricate your feelings about the work. Be kind, thorough and constructive.

Go easy on the writer, but not on the writing.

ASKING THE **RIGHT QUESTIONS**

By now you'll probably have gathered that one of the main skills a script editor needs to develop is learning to ask the right questions. Asking the right questions while assessing the script, asking the right questions while discussing the script with the writer, and asking the right questions when the writer is feeling blocked or stuck. Asking the right questions is the key to analysing and solving most script and story problems.

Knowing what to ask comes with experience over time, but much of it is also plain logic. Once you know how the building blocks of story work it becomes easier to ask the right questions and easier to help writers organise their ideas and follow through with their vision for their story.

Throughout this book I have made a point of highlighting questions that I consider important each step of the way. Here are some others for you to consider. These are questions I ask when I am examining a screenplay. I hope they will help guide you deeper into the thought process of assessing a script.

What are the themes of the script?
Are they apparent or is clarity needed?

Writers need to establish the theme of their film early on. What message are they trying to convey? Love conquers all? Good versus Evil? An underdog triumphs? Whatever it is – it needs to be set up from the very start.

What is the world of the story?
Is it clear and does it remain consistent?

As the story begins, we are entering a world. Where does the story take place? What is different and interesting about the world of the story? What are the rules in the world of the script? Here again, the set-up should start right away and the rules of the world must remain consistent.

Does the story open in a strong way?

Having a clear and powerful opening is essential. The sooner the audience understands the kind of story they are viewing the sooner they will relax and engage. Openings should provide a sense of tone, mood, place, texture, character, and can potentially even introduce the theme of the script.

Consider this opening:

A young couple run to the beach and towards the sea on a beautiful moonlit evening – undressing as they go. The woman dives in and we see the silhouette of her body from under the water as she swims, enjoying the tranquillity of the evening. Suddenly she is pulled under. Attacked and killed by an unknown monster.

That opening from *Jaws* sets the tone of the film right away and makes it very clear what kind of story is about to unfold.

Take a look at the openings of your favourite films. Observe how they progress – and notice how much information is being conveyed at the very beginning.

Some questions to consider:

- Is the story original?

- Is the premise creative?

- Are the themes strong? Is there also a moral message?

- Do the themes come across naturally or are they too obvious and forced?

- Is the structure of the script well constructed?

- Are the first ten pages of the script engaging?

- Does the story start at the latest possible point it can?

- Is the story question clear?

- Where and when does the story take place?

- What is the genre of the script?

- Does the story work within the genre the writer has chosen?

- Does the first act set up the rest of the story?

- Does the first act set up the conflict of the story?

- Is there a clear inciting incident?

- Does the script contain enough conflict and obstacles in the second act to sustain interest?

- Do each of the turning points increase the stakes and reaffirm the story question?

- Does the third act tie up all the loose ends and provide a satisfying resolution?

- Do the subplots add dimension to the main story?

- Do the subplots have structure – their own beginning, middle and end?

- Does the second-act turning point lead the character into the third act?

- Is there a unique voice and tone to the story?

- Is the climax as intense as it should be?

- Does the title given to the script convey the essence of the story?
- Is the story predictable or unpredictable?
- What is the pace of the story?
- What is the tone of the story?
- Does the story evoke some emotion?
- Would the story work better if set in an alternative time or location?
- Does the main character grow and change?
- Is it clear what the main character wants/needs?
- Do I understand what is driving them to do what they are doing?
- Are the characters well developed?
- Is the protagonist sympathetic?
- Do I care about any of the characters?
- Are there enough or too many characters in the story?
- Is it easy to keep track of which character is which within the story?
- Do the characters have their own unique and distinctive voices?
- Are the supporting characters sufficiently developed?
- Is it clear what the antagonist wants?
- Are the relationships between the characters well developed?
- Are the characters believable? Stereotypical? Understandable?
- Does the main character have distinctive flaws?
- Would the roles in the script be appealing for actors/actresses?
- Are the characters original?
- Is the protagonist a hero?
- Is the protagonist a victim?

- Is the protagonist an 'everyman' type of person going about their business?

- Is their main conflict internal or external?

- What kind of journey are they on?

- Where do they begin their journey and where do they end up?

- Is the conflict clearly defined?

- Is the goal achieved?

- Within the realm of the story, is the story believable?

- Is the plot overly complicated or understandable?

- Is the dialogue engaging?

- Can any of the dialogue be replaced with a gesture, an action or a look?

- Is the writer telling rather than showing the story?

- Do all of the scenes move the story forward?

- Is there enough visual grammar in the script?

- Do each of the scenes begin and end at the best possible moment in the story (omitting all information that is not relevant to the story)?

- Are the scenes entertaining?

- Are the scenes visual enough?

- Are any of the scenes repetitive?

- What is the purpose of each scene?

- Is the conflict and objective of each scene clear?

- Are the locations well chosen in each of the scenes?

- Are the descriptions concise and visual?

- Does each scene transition into the next?

- Are the scenes of varying length – allowing for good pacing?
- Does the premise have commercial appeal?
- Will the story appeal to a wide audience?
- Can the script make a successful movie?

Answering story, character, element and content questions will give you the information you need to plan a strong and useful set of development notes.

Remember to prioritise, giving only what is useful in each session, but keeping track of how to progress as needed.

TREATMENTS, OUTLINES AND PITCHING **MATERIALS**

We've discussed how writing a premise, premise line, synopsis and logline can greatly help with the development process, but it's important to remember that these same materials are also a critical part of the business side of the trade. These documents are used constantly after the script is polished and ready to be read by potential agents and producers. It is essential that at this stage all pitching documents are revised and strengthened to present the work in its best possible light.

There are thousands of writers looking to be produced, and piquing the interest of any potential backer is of great importance. It's often difficult for writers to sell themselves or to distil their own work down to pitch size – and it can become even harder seeing things clearly if it's been in development for ages. Writers often need assistance with these fundamental pitching tools – and frequently it falls upon the script editor to help guide them in how to craft pitch documents that will best represent the project and the screenwriter themselves.

Suggestions for pitch documents:

- Make pitch documents easy on the eyes. Overly dense paragraphs and pages tend to make people cringe – better to be concise, keep the pace moving and leave the reader wanting to know more.

- Film is a visual medium – the more you can 'show' the reader what the script is, the better. Find visual elements that create pictures in the reader's mind – but be brief. You have to keep the documents tight.

- Include colourful descriptions and details that make the script sound and feel exciting.

- Writers need their pitch materials to demonstrate mastery of the craft. Make sure that they express a clear idea about what the story is – and that their synopsis provides clearly defined characters with a solid story that contains a beginning, middle and end.

- Writers often resist this, but it's usually best to satisfy the reader by giving away the ending. If they don't know how it ends, the reader will not know how to react to the story, and that will make it difficult to evoke strong feelings about the material (other than frustration at not knowing how it ends).

- Pitching materials should be critiqued by two different kinds of readers before sending them out professionally. First, by the same people who have read and developed the scripts – because if a person has not read the script, how can they confirm that the pitching materials truly represent it? And secondly, by a completely independent reader, because fresh eyes will help make it clear if the materials are exciting and going to generate interest.

- Let the reader know what kind of setting the story/screenplay takes place in. Give them both the time and place, along with a little bit of background information.

- Use third person to tell the story in three acts, i.e. follow the order of the story/screenplay.

- Make sure the present tense is being used to write the synopsis.

- Make sure the main characters are briefly described as they appear in the story.

- Make sure that any key or important scenes and culminating events are included.

- Suggest that writers resist including any dialogue from the script unless absolutely necessary.

- Be sure that the writer has tied up any loose ends at the conclusion.

These next points may sound obvious, but I've seen them missed out on too many occasions not to mention them:

- Make sure that the title of the project and the name of the writer are clearly listed at the top of the page.

- Provide a heading that informs the reader what they are about to read – make it clear what pitch documents are included.

- Don't forget to include contact information. Yes, believe it or not, people do sometimes forget!

REVISITING THE SYNOPSIS – FOR PITCHING PURPOSES

What was explained about synopses in the script report section remains true for the development documents. However, there are some minor differences, as these will now be used to either inspire creative interest or acquire funding.

WRITING AN EFFECTIVE SYNOPSIS PITCH

- Still limit the synopsis to three paragraphs.

- Remember the synopsis does not try to tell the whole story, but focuses on the most important parts.

- Make sure the synopsis is written in the most interesting way possible.

- Incorporate a taste of the style of the writing into the synopsis – so that the reader will see the tone of the script emerging through the writing of the synopsis.

- A good synopsis will make the reader want to take action! If they want to see the script made into a movie, they will be more inclined to help make that happen.

- Secondary characters can be introduced, but don't make the synopsis too detailed.

- Include the most important conflict or events in the story.

- Use the present tense.

- Write synopsis paragraphs in a logical way, so they tell the story and flow together.

- Include a sentence or two about the ending scenes and how the story concludes.

Does your synopsis...

- Give an accurate view of the story?

- Make it easy to pitch to others?

- Lend itself to being easily understood? (Or is it overly complicated, containing too many unnecessary details?)

If the answer is NOT YES to all of the above questions, continue working on it!

LOGLINE QUESTIONS

- Does the logline convey the story in a clear, CONCISE way while also being engaging?

- Are the word choices descriptive and do they evoke the GENRE and TONE?

- Is the logline written in an ACTIVE VOICE?

- When I pitch my logline DO EYES LIGHT UP OR GLAZE OVER?

- That last one is important. Is the listener intrigued? That's the goal. You've succeeded when they want to hear more or ask to read your script.

TREATMENTS AND OUTLINES

What is an outline and how does it differ from a synopsis or a treatment?

As we've discussed, a synopsis is generally defined as a descriptive narrative of what happens in your story, told in a very concise manner, and with care (and flair), as it will eventually be used as a selling tool to entice an agent, publisher or producer to read the manuscript.

A film treatment is a different beast. A treatment can be used as a tool to pitch an upcoming script that the writer is working on. It generally consists of 20 to 40 or more pages of narrative that go into detail about the story. Over the years treatments have changed quite a bit and, in Hollywood now, they are much shorter than they used to be, ranging from four to ten pages (many would suggest that the shorter the better but twenty pages is the average.) So the lines between treatments and synopses have become somewhat blurred.

The key thing to understand is that a synopsis is a three-paragraph description of the script, whereas a treatment is a longer, more detailed script proposal.

An outline is a completely different tool, although writers do sometimes use treatments as a method of outlining and planning their scripts.

Outlines can take many different forms, but the purpose of an outline is to provide a breakdown of how a story will play out. This can be organised in various ways based on the writer's needs and way of thinking. Writers tend to acquire their own methods of outlining or breaking down their stories. Some do it by beats, others scene by scene or by structural elements such as the opening, inciting incident and three-act structure. The length and amount of detail in an outline will vary, and the style is individual to each writer. Some are handwritten, some are computer-generated, and some writers choose to write the major beats down on file cards that they can arrange and rearrange as they work. Different factors, including purpose, level of detail, method of creation, and writer preference, will determine how the outline is structured as they are usually intended for the writer's own use as a map of their story and not intended to be shared.

Many writers use outlines – some do not.

I have witnessed first-hand that working from an outline, be it for a novel, a play or a screenplay, generally saves time and improves the writer's productivity. So, for the sake of time and efficiency, when appropriate, I do recommend that writers work with one. And, yes, I've heard the argument that the outlining process can deplete creativity and spontaneity, but I've not personally witnessed that. I have only seen it help writers take control of their writing. It aids them in knowing what is working and what isn't working and in seeing how to fix the problems that do exist with greater ease. It's a thousand times easier to fix a problem at the outline stage than after the script has been written!

Outlines are safe places for writers to construct, deconstruct and rework their stories. Without a framework, it is much easier to over or underwrite portions of the script. It's easy to lose track of where the story is meant to be going if the writer hasn't done the groundwork – in part because the writer may not have made the important choices that will eventually shape the story. But a bit of thoughtful preparation is usually time well spent. There are many pieces of the puzzle that can go awry: entire characters may be written unnecessarily, confusing character arcs or character motivations may muddy the waters of the story, there may be scenes within the script that work against the rest of the narrative and its themes. The worst part is that once big changes start being implemented in the script, the total structure risks falling apart because any one element impacts the others. An outline will normally help writers avoid these kinds of troubles.

Nevertheless, some writers prefer a more spontaneous approach and this is truly a personal choice. A script editor must not impose their methods or ideas on a writer, but adapt to how their clients prefer to work. They must also be prepared to offer assistance should the writer become lost or confused in the process. That said, in my experience (and please understand this is a generalisation), for the most part writers working without a plan often results in work that is muddled or imbalanced. Too often scripts will be abandoned entirely because the writer has become stuck or discouraged. Without a strategy, a great deal of time can be wasted solving problems that would have been spotted early on – if an outline had been prepared.

An outline will enable the writer to critically review each scene and determine how it fits into the whole of the story. They will be able to see how they've paced the story, where it sags and needs help, and where it rushes through important beats. They will be able to better consider their character choices – the character arcs and motivations. It will help them: balance the tone, make sure the story question is being reinforced, make sure there isn't a great deal of repetition taking place, that the scenes have enough happening and are focused, that the story makes sense and is compelling, and that the scenes are being set up properly for the audience. It gives the writer a chance to be objective and have a bit of distance to consider whether all the pieces are working together and determine if there is enough at stake, enough edge, comedy or heart, depending on the genre. And again, it's much easier to fix things at this stage! With few exceptions, a writer working without a plan usually proves to be less effective than one who takes the time to work things out before they start writing dialogue.

Can it be done? Yes.

Is it a script editor's job to impose a process that forces the writer to create an outline?

No. Not unless it is part of a specific job or brief.

Television and film scripts written on assignment rather than on spec (meaning a screenplay written purely in the hope that it will one day be sold, but which is non-contracted) often require an outline. In these circumstances the outline will invariably be read by producers, studio or network executives and development staff, and should therefore be written with that in mind.

Outlining can be rather daunting and, for those unfamiliar with the process, it may seem difficult to understand what is involved. There is not a specific style or formula and writers develop their own types. To give you an idea of how some writers do this, I have included a few samples.

These outlines were written by John August for his screenplay *Big Fish*.

BIG FISH OUTLINE

As you will see, in this outline John August has written one sentence to depict each of the main beats in each act of the film.

NOTE: The initials refer to characters. The character key is below.

ACT ONE
'On The Day He Was Born....'
Opening Titles: Will grows, Edward annoys
France: Will gets the call (J)
Airplane: Fly to Alabama (J)
The Snowstorm (M,F,E)
Arrive at house: Meet the mother, Dr. Bennett (S, B, J, W)
First Will/Edward talk (W&E)
The Giant (Karl)
Will wants one real conversation: 'A stranger I know very well' (W&J)
Sandra asks Will to go through papers (S, W)
The Girl In The River (Girl)
The Day He Left Ashland (M, F, E, K)
The Town On The Road (E)

ACT TWO
Edward tells Josephine (E, J)
The Old Lady and the Eye: meet Don (Don)
Meet Sandra (S)

Woo Sandra (K, S, D)
Fight Don (Don)
Second Will/Edward Conversation (W, E)
He Goes to War (D, K, China the 2-headed woman)
Josephine in labor (W, J, B)
The Day Will was born (B, S, W)
Will argues with Edward (E, W)
Edward into coma (S, B, E)

ACT THREE
Will finds deed; mistress; she loved Edward's stories (W)
Mistress tells: He Traveled the World (E)
Mistress tells: In which He Buys a House (E)
Will confronts Sandra about the affair; of course she knew. Assume I'm Stupid? (W, S)
Edward awakes, peace making, not understandiing (W, E)
Edward dies (W, E)
Funeral, guest (Don, Karl, 2-headed Woman)
At the grave with son (W, J, Kid)
Big Fish (Everyone)
'That's Funny' (W, J, Kid)

Character key:
W = Will, E = Edward, S = Sandra, J = Josephine, K = Karl,
M = Edward's Mother, F = Edward's Father

BIG FISH SEQUENCE OUTLINE

In the next outline, which is a sequence outline, John has numbered the sequences, estimated a page count, given the sequence a title, and included a very concise description of what takes place in each sequence.

Seq. 01 – Pages 1–6 – The Catfish.
Edward tells the same big fish story throughout Will's life, finishing at Will's wedding. Will and Edward have an argument.

Seq. 02 – Pages 6–8 – Those Three Years.
The next three years pass. Will's voiceover explains how he and his father communicated indirectly. Edward swims; Will and Josephine check on the health of their unborn child.

Seq. 03 – Pages 8–11 – The Day My Father Was Born.
Will tells the story of the day his father was born, the day it finally rained in Ashland.

Seq. 04 – Pages 11–14 – Will gets the phone call.
Will gets word that his father's condition has worsened. He and Josephine board a plane for the States.

Seq. 05 – Pages 14–23 – The Old Lady and The Eye.
Retrieving a toy plane, Edward is caught by the one-eyed old woman, who will only give him the plane if he returns her glass eye, stolen by Don Price. She warns him not to look into the eye, for in it he will see the last moments of his life. Edward manipulates Don and his friend into looking into The Eye, scaring them off. Too curious not to, Edward looks into The Eye himself. Armed with the foreknowledge of his own passing, Edward never fears death.

Seq. 06 – Pages 23–27 – Will Returns Home.
Will and Josephine arrive. We meet Sandra Bloom and Doctor Bennett.

Seq. 07 – Pages 27–30 – Will talks with Edward.
The first time we've seen ill Edward. He and Will talk.

Seq. 08 – Pages 30–37 – Edward and the Giant Leave Ashland.
Will tells the story of his father and Karl the Giant. When the townsfolk organize a lynch-mob to stop the menace, Edward volunteers to try to talk sense into Karl. He ends up convincing Karl to leave Ashland with him.

Seq. 09 – Pages 37–48 – The Town of Spectre.
The First Time splitting from Karl at a fork in the road, Edward finds himself in Spectre, a town full of people who can never leave, including Beaman, Norther Winslow, Piano Phil and Baton Woman.

Edward tries to leave Spectre ten separate times in ten separate directions, but each time finds himself back where he started. He asks a mysterious Girl in the river how to leave. She points to him and says the answer is in him – he knows how. Edward discovers what has been keeping Spectre's inhabitants hostage; they keep repeating the same mistakes. He's able to walk backwards out of town.

Seq. 10 – Pages 48–50 – A Mysterious Woman at the Winn-Dixie.
Will and his mother shop for groceries. They lightly discuss the rift between Will and his father. A beautiful blonde woman keeps looking at Will. Does he know her?

Seq. 11 – Pages 50–54 – Edward and Josephine.
Edward tells Josephine about his portentous dream, then explains he's always had that ability. His story turns into a Milk Man joke. Edward tells her the story of how he met, wooed, and won Sandra.

Seq. 12 – Pages 54–66 – The Circus and his Many Labors.
Edward and Karl visit a circus where Karl dwarfs the main attraction. Edward sees a beautiful girl and falls in love. Amos Calloway knows who it is, but doesn't think Edward is worthy. Edward convinces Amos to let him work for information about this girl – he's madly in love with. Edward completes Amos's tasks, each more difficult than the last, each time getting one more piece of information about the love of his life. Finally, Edward plays fetch with Amos – a kind of werewolf. Amos, grateful, gives Edward the final piece of information. The girl's name is Sandra Templeton and she goes to Auburn.

Seq. 13 – Pages 66–73 – The College and The Fight.
Edward attempts to court Sandra but discovers that not only does he already know her, (she was Sandy back in Ashland) but unfortunately he's too late. She's engaged to wed Don Price. Edward doesn't give up, continuing to profess his love in every manner possible. Don Price arrives and beats a passive Edward within an inch of his life. Sandra dumps Don and agrees to go out with Edward. Don Price, true to his destiny, falls off the toilet, dead.

Seq. 14 - Page 74 - But Wait There's More.
Josephine asks again, why didn't Edward and Sandra have a full wedding? He continues the story.

Seq. 15 - Pages 75-81 - The War.
Before Sandra and Edward can marry, he is drafted into the Army. He volunteers for the most dangerous assignments to shorten his tour. He parachutes into an enemy USO-type show where he meets Ping and Jing who, after hearing of his love for Sandra, let Edward join them as they escape the country for the United Sates. Edward returns home to Sandra.

Seq. 16 - Pages 81-83 - In Bed with Will and Josephine.
Will explains that he doesn't truly know anything about his father, only tall tales and stories with punch lines.

Seq. 17 - Pages 83-85 - Breakfast.
Over breakfast Will tries to talk with his father about what, if anything, he truly believes. Will gets a Jesus/Pinocchio joke for his troubles.

Seq. 18 - Pages 85-89 - Will's Chores, and his Discovery.
Will takes out the trash and skims the family pool, which apparently has a monster in it. In the cluttered garage, Will goes through his father's old papers. Discovering a property loan application, Will heads off to investigate.

Seq. 19 - Pages 89-93 - Will meets Jenny Hill.
Will arrives at Jenny Hill's house. She explains how she and Edward met.

Seq. 20 - Pages 93-104 - Edward Buys A Town.
Caught in a deluge, Edward finds himself back in Spectre. Falling in love with it, he buys up all of Spectre except for one small shack in the swamp, which belongs to Jenny Hill. Edward tries to buy Jenny's land, but she won't sell. After mistakenly breaking her front door, Edward starts to repair the entire home. Jenny falls in love with Edward and the two begin their relationship. People in the town look at Edward

in a different light he's no longer an outsider, but rather a part of the community. Edward leaves the town and as Jenny waits and waits for him to return, her house is taken over by the swamp, transforming into the Old Woman's house from the beginning of the story.

Seq. 21 – Pages 104–105 – What Jenny Tells Will.
Finished with her account of the story, Jenny tells Will about how proud his father was of him, and how envious she was of him.

Seq. 22 – Pages 105–108 – Turn for the Worse.
Will returns home to find the house empty. At the hospital, he learns Edward has had a stroke.

Seq. 23 – Pages 108–111 – The Hospital.
Dr. Bennett tells Will the real story of Will's birth. Will makes a list of all his father's stories. When Will wakes the next morning, he finds Edward has died.

Seq. 24 – Pages 112–116 – The Funeral.
At the service, the 'real' versions of many of the characters from Edward's tall tales arrive to pay their respects. As his father's last wish, Will tells the story about the cat on the roof.

Seq. 25 – Page 116 – Jumping Ahead.
Will tells his young son the story of his Grandfather's death.

Seq. 26 – Pages 116–122 – Edward's Death, the Funny Version.
Will wakes in the hospital to find Edward sitting up in bed getting dressed. They escape the hospital, racing to the banks of the Ashland River. There a crowd of more than a hundred waits – including most of the faces we've met along the way. Edward says his good-byes as Will carries him into the water. There Edward turns into a catfish and swims away.

Seq. 27 – Pages 122–123 – How it Ends.
Will, Josephine and their Son leave the cemetery. The Son wants to hear more stories about his grandfather.

A helpful exercise would be to watch *Big Fish*, directed by Tim Burton, and notice how the outlines correspond to the scenes in the film. This will give you a very strong sense of how the outlines have worked and inform you how you can help writers create them for their screenplays.

Treatments and outlines mean different things to different people; one writer's treatment might be another's outline and vice versa.

TREATMENTS

Treatments are widely used within the industry as selling documents to outline story and character aspects of a planned screenplay, whereas outlines are generally produced as part of the development of the screenplay. Traditionally, treatments are written in prose and read like a short story, but are told in the present tense and describe events as they happen. Outlines are more like breakdowns or scene lists with just slug lines to refer to sequences. However, this will vary depending on the writer's style.

Treatments usually contain a full description of a story covering character, plot, setting and theme and may also include detailed character descriptions, a synopsis and statements on theme and tone. A treatment should clarify the intent of the writer and attempt to convey the movie from beginning to end.

Screenwriters may use a treatment to initially pitch a screenplay, but may also use a treatment to sell a concept they are pitching without a completed screenplay.

An outline might be one page or ten; a treatment could be three pages or thirty – it just depends on the writer. James Cameron is known for blending the two and writing 'script-ments'. His scriptment for *Titanic* was 131 pages long.

Ultimately, the function of both treatments and outlines is to map out the movie story, often as a precursor to writing the full screenplay. This allows the writer to summarise the script before writing a draft and catch problems early on.

EXERCISES

This is an exercise that most film-school students are assigned, no matter which department they are in. It is geared to teaching them how films are constructed. It's very informative, and if you have never done it, I suggest that you give it a try.

Watch a DVD of a film or show that interests you. View the first scene, and then pause it. Write a few lines (three or four) saying what the scene was about. Then play the second scene, and repeat the process. Continue this until you have done the entire film or programme. At the end of the exercise, you will have an outline for that story. This exercise will help give you an understanding of what the writer was doing, and how they constructed the script.

Another exercise that is also very informative is to complete the same process, but without having the sound on. Concentrating on just the images is another very valuable way of learning how a film is constructed. Films are visual stories, meant to be shown and not told. Pick a few of your favourite films and watch them with the volume turned off – consider how the images are being used to tell the story. What devices are being used to convey the information without it having to be said?

Any tool that helps to inform how a script works is of value. Ultimately, it is about breaking the story down into workable, understandable and meaningful pieces of the story puzzle and mapping out the writer's ideas, and how those ideas will be best communicated in the screenplay. Remember – everyone has their own way of working and it is a very personal choice as to which tools prove useful for an individual. This can only be determined on a project by project (writer by writer) basis.

SCRIPT EDITING FOR **TELEVISION**

Just as each project is individual, each medium is also different and there are varied ways of working within them. The job of script editing changes somewhat depending on which media format you are working in. This chapter will explain how the script editor's job shifts depending on the writer's and project's needs during development and production.

Artistic differences between cinema and television used to be vast, but TV has come such a long way that now those differences are far less great. Still, when working on a script, choosing which medium to write for remains as important as ever. Projects take such a long time to develop and get green-lit that it can be very disheartening – especially for the writer. Television does still have the advantage (and challenge) of moving a bit faster than film.

In film, writers are typically allowed to work at their own pace within reason, and even if their script is incredibly strong it can take many months or even years to get it off the ground as financing becomes harder and harder to obtain. In TV, the time scale is notably accelerated – which means the turnover time between drafts can be extremely quick.

As we know, the script editor acts as the liaison between the writer and the production. A large part of the job is problem solving, finding ways around research or production issues and helping find ways to make it possible to tell the story the writer wants to write – while also meeting the deadline. It's the script editor's task to creatively energise and motivate the writer to do the best job they possibly can, and to develop strategies to enable the writer to do their finest work. Both writer and script editor have to incorporate the many considerations of production – the realities of limited budgets and time, location and cast availability, difficult executive notes, etc. – and work positively within all of those challenges.

Once the writer is hired, a script editor will be their main point of contact. In a perfect world, all notes will go directly to the script editor who will then condense, arrange and prioritise them before communicating them to the writer. The script editor will provide a single, coherent and consistent set of notes to the writer on every draft, outline, treatment and script. Sometimes, however, it's not a perfect world and notes get through to the writer from other sources – this is not ideal because things go wrong when too many voices give notes. Try to stop this from happening by explaining the necessity of a unified front, but if you are working with producers or directors who tend to give notes directly to the writer, try to be present at those meetings so that you are aware of what is being communicated. The last thing a writer needs is conflicting notes. So, speak with anyone giving the writer notes and at least ensure that they are also communicating them to you.

The core of the script editing process is reading scripts, making notes, getting notes from other members of the creative/editorial team and then briefing the writer. This cycle happens quicker and more frequently in television, and you will often be working on four to six episodes at a time. That means taking each of those episodes through revisions, which can be up to six drafts (depending on the show). In addition to that, you will have to read drafts from everyone else's episodes to ensure continuity is intact, as well as reading scripts from agents and writers to stay up to date with talent.

Unlike film, series television follows a prescribed format, whether it's a serial, a sitcom or a one-hour drama. There are often definite act breaks to allow for adverts, and the overall framework of television shows tends to limit what kinds of stories can occur within an individual programme. Traditionally, each episode usually has a limited number of recurring characters and sets available and the production restrictions are greater. Television writing is generally more collaborative (especially in the US), with a group of writers contributing to that week's script, under the supervision of a producer called the 'showrunner'. The pace of television writing is much faster than film writing, because there's a continuous need to keep up with production. This means that story ideas get swallowed up, and storylines tend to be drawn out, as the need for content is continuous.

Film has far fewer limits on structure, storyline, characters and tone. It's also usually much more solitary work because, aside from the script editor and occasional producer meetings, the writer is away doing the writing on their own – and that can take months or even years.

Working on an episode of a drama series or serial, the writing process from initial pitch to shooting script can sometimes last many months, but it can also be as short as a couple of weeks. On a series, a big part of the script editor's job is to communicate to the writers the serial, continuity and 'house-style' concerns they need to acknowledge in their scripts and to make sure the writers keep to a tight schedule.

Script editors are often responsible for significant and in-depth research for stories and storylines, working both independently as needed and also alongside experts and advisors. In the crime drama *Above Suspicion*, our main advisor was an ex-policeman and forensics expert. He became an invaluable source to bounce story ideas off, and made sure our police, forensics and protocol details were accurate for the series. It is common for shows to have experts, be they medical, crime, legal or any other specialised topic in need of intense detail. It's important for the accuracy of the show's content, and it is most often the script editor who coordinates those details with the advisors.

Experts know their field, but they don't necessarily know the show, and it often takes a lot of finesse to find a satisfying compromise between how a story plot is being written and what the experts suggest gets changed. Often discussions revolve around how to

121

maintain a realistic storyline while also keeping it interesting and dramatic. Here again, it is essential to be collaborative and respectful in order to obtain the best results for the show.

Another vital and exciting part of the job is creating the over-arching serial storylines with the editorial team. For many serials there are at least four script editors working at once. Each one is given a block of scripts to oversee and through a succession of meetings the story and character arcs of the show will be decided on and developed.

Each writer pitches a few stories for the episodes they would like to write for, which is often a set of five for a full week. These pitches are then discussed and the ones best suited for the show will be selected. The writers are then informed of the serial beats they need to include in each of their episodes and they then go on to write a treatment for each of the episodes. During these meetings the journeys of the plot and character arcs will be worked out. If something isn't working the script editor will point that out to the writer and work with them until they are in sync with the editorial team and the show. Fixes done at the treatment stage will save important time and reduce headaches later. Once the treatment is complete the writer will proceed to writing the script, scene by scene, working through notes at each stage.

The storylines might shift slightly in the writing and development of the episodes, but it is important to have a clear plan to pass on to the other series writers. Communication between the other writers and script editors is of the utmost importance as any small detail changed can impact another's storyline. The series editor will check for consistency of characters, continuity of storylines and examine each character's arc through the production process.

As the shoot approaches, the number of people contributing to the notes increases. For example, locations might have to be shifted due to scheduling or budgeting constraints, or an actor might become ill, resulting in a storyline having to be adjusted or rescheduled. These challenges can force the writer and editor to focus on the essentials of the story and it is often these kinds of restrictions that inspire the most interesting work. This is also true for feature film. Many times it is the bigger-budget films, with the greater resources, that fall short creatively; somehow being able to do almost anything stifles the innovative process and causes a lack of focus. Things can get too big, losing their direction and importance.

The relationship between the script editor and writer requires trust on both sides. Under normal circumstances, the relationship will develop gradually and a mutual respect will grow. But under intense deadlines things can feel forced. Each project has its own needs and it is important that the participants involved remain flexible, focused and respectful. The job of a writer can be isolating, so it's important that they feel the script editor is accessible. The script editor must also stay in touch, keeping the writer informed of all production issues pertaining to their scripts without overdoing it or disturbing their progress.

Note-giving is a delicate job and it is important that you do it with respect and care.

Shows can have as many as 25 writers working on them per season (in the United States this is very standard). In the UK this happens primarily on soaps such as *Casualty*. More writers means more personalities, opinions and working styles to deal with, and it's the script editor's job to coordinate all the producer and director notes and relay them in a clear, sensible and respectful way. It's crucial to have good working relationships with the writers as the most effective work happens when there is clear communication and trust.

You want the writer to be supported and not on the defensive. How you give a note is important; it's so much easier if you are able to explain the note clearly and logically so that the writer is able to understand the idea at the heart of it. It's very difficult when a writer can't relate to the idea or resists the process and only passively participates without really connecting to the idea. The only way forward is through healthy communication geared towards supporting the writer's vision of the work.

Once you get to know a writer you will find the technique that complements their temperament, allowing you to develop good communication between you.

STORYLINE CYCLES

Working on soaps is equivalent to script boot camp for a script editor and writer. It is ultra-fast-paced work and exceedingly chaotic. There is a fast turnover in soaps because it is extremely hard work and many individuals only last a few months in the trenches – but it is a wonderful way to gain extensive experience.

Each television show has its own cycles and way of working. The more shows per week being produced, the more hectic the process becomes. For shows that run five times a week (*EastEnders*, *Emmerdale* and *Coronation Street*) the schedule is truly gruelling and writers are expected to deliver a first draft within two weeks of signing their contracts. What makes it even more complex for the script editor is that they are working on up to five scripts at a time and each of them is at different stages of the process. One may be shooting, one may be a production draft, one may be at the first-draft stage, and the others may be outlines or in various draft forms.

On shows of this nature there are generally no more than five drafts done before the shooting script is required (sometimes only three drafts are permissible, depending on the schedule). These shows have been running for years and are amazingly efficient – but each person must work at full capacity for months and months at a time.

A typical week on a soap is generally working on a monthly cycle. For script editors, the days usually start at 9 am and the first things done are reviewing the script, preparing the edits and contacting the writers. The week will usually alternate between editing treatments, various drafts, rehearsal scripts and shooting scripts. Each week tends to consist of a reading day, a script meeting where scripts are reviewed page by page, the preparation of edits, and the script editor contacting the writers with the notes. Headline notes are discussed on story changes, as are character through-lines and continuity, and then a page by page script review with the writer as needed.

Script editors on soaps tend to do about three edits a day, and when a script is filming they will also get calls and questions and must be available for any on-set script issues. The script editor will get regular updates on the timings as they will often have to look for cuts or additional material as needed.

Shows tend to work on blocks of three, four or five scripts at a time. This means having multiple scripts at multiple stages simultaneously. When scripts are shooting, the script editors are on call from around 7 am to 7 pm every day for any on-set issues and queries. They may also be called on outside of these hours if needed. On soaps and some serials there may also be an assistant script editor and one or two part-time series script editors working throughout.

The script editor must know what the vision is for the series, the episode, and the story arcs. They must know the concept of the show and its overall structure and set-up. They must know the history of the show and characters well – for example, how the characters have evolved and what they have experienced. They must protect and maintain story and character continuity and the style of the show, and within all that help the writers find new and inventive ways of keeping the storylines and characters interesting.

STORYLINERS

Some shows have a separate team of storyliners as well as a story producer and story editor. Stories are generated every month at a story meeting and the storyliners independently write story strands and then a storyline document is produced. The writers and producers use the storyline document when reading first drafts to see what the intention of the story was, and to understand any decisions the writer has made, to check that all story beats are covered.

SCRIPT DRAFTS

This system is used for both feature films and in television.

Once a treatment has been approved the next step for the writer is to write the first draft. The drafts and revisions are colour-coded (printed on coloured paper) to ensure that the writers, editors and production team know what stage of the script each draft is.

The colour codes may vary from show to show depending on the production, but they are typically as follows:

- *First drafts are white.* At this stage the script editor will assess the draft and have a meeting with the producers to compile all their notes. The script editor will then (in a clear and supportive way) communicate those notes to the writer with the goal of helping them focus, prioritise and proceed quickly and succinctly. At this stage of a script, notes will probably be extensive; the script editor will be reviewing all the areas of the script and giving detailed notes to ensure that the second draft progresses quickly and well.

  There are also many practical considerations that will be reviewed here in terms of production, locations, scheduling, timing, etc. There may be a need for additional research, or to adjust for continuity issues. Again, each show has its own needs and requirements and a script editor must be flexible and learn how the show they have joined works – and quickly! In all cases, the aim of the process at this stage is to get the writer ready for a second draft, by providing the notes necessary to clear out any problem areas, sort out any issues, provide research as needed, and help tighten up and streamline the storylines, getting the scenes closer to the length needed for the show.

- *Second drafts are blue.* This draft should now be cleaner and closer to what is required for the show. By this point, continuity issues should have been addressed, commercial breaks should be incorporated for the broadcasters that need them, and any structural problems and timing issues should be sorted – or at least greatly improved. This draft will again undergo notes and at this point the focus is usually on dialogue, dramatic content, and pace and subtext.

- *Third drafts are pink.* This is the final draft before the script becomes a rehearsal script. At this point the director will join in to contribute their notes to the process. The script editor will work together with the writer, director and producers on whatever adjustments are needed at this point. Once those changes are made the script will be passed on to either the director's PA or to the script coordinator for distribution to the cast, department heads and production team.

- *Rehearsal scripts are white*. These are used at the table read, which is an important gathering that includes the cast, director, producers and executives, writer, heads of department and the script editor. This is when the script or script blocks of episodes are read aloud. Following the readings, the cast will usually be released and there will be a script meeting, during which any problems, whether creative, editorial, financial or production-related, are addressed.

  Hopefully, by this stage, script problems will be minimal. Often the biggest concern at this point is how long the show is running – whether it is too long or too short. Typically scripts spread, meaning that they run a bit longer than expected and cuts will be needed, but sometimes the script will be too short and additional material will need to be written to fill the script out. (This is considered more problematic as trimming a scene is much easier than trying to build one up.) Also, at this time, any unsatisfying dialogue will be cleaned up and any other minor issues should be addressed via the writer and script editor. Once that is done, the draft is signed off by the producers in preparation for the shooting script.

- *The shooting script*. At this stage the coordinator/script supervisor/ production assistants usually liaise with the script editor about script distribution needs and show timings. Scripts at this point must be clean and ready to go. They must have the correct number of allocated interior and exterior scenes and be close to the proper running time.

If revisions have been necessary since the rehearsal script they will be incorporated on blue pages – and so the process continues; the next set of revisions will be on pink, and so on. By the time the show is done filming, the shooting script may be filled with various coloured pages. It's important that the sequence be kept in order and that the page colour be listed in the header of the script alongside the date, for example, 'Show Title 9/21/15 Revisions (PINK)'.

The standard script-revision colour sets are as follows:

- Blue revision
- Pink revision
- Yellow revision
- Green revision
- Goldenrod revision
- Buff revision
- Salmon revision
- Cherry revision

If this cycle has been used and more revisions are necessary, the cycle starts again. Pages are then called either 'double' or 'second' blue revision, pink revision, etc.

- Second (or double) blue revision
- Second (or double) pink revision
- Second (or double) yellow revision
- Second (or double) green revision
- Second (or double) goldenrod revision
- Second (or double) buff revision
- Second (or double) salmon revision
- Second (or double) cherry revision

SCRIPT REVISIONS – PRESERVING SCENE AND PAGE NUMBERS

When a screenplay (or TV script) is approved for production, the scenes are assigned numbers, which are listed in the script alongside the scene headers. The scene numbers provide a convenient way for the various production departments to reference individual scenes.

After a shooting script has been circulated, page numbers are LOCKED, and any revisions that follow are distributed on revision pages correlating to those page numbers. In other words, if the production office has to issue revisions on script page 25 then only that page will be reissued. The page numbers must remain the same so they can flow sequentially into the pre-existing page numbers.

If the revision made on page 25 makes the scene longer and now occupies two and a half pages, the revisions will be distributed on three pages numbered 25, 25A, 25B (and so on as needed). This system makes it easy for the scene to be replaced within the bulk of the script and without disturbing other page numbers. Conversely, if pages 24 and 25 are shortened such that they now occupy a single page, the revisions will be distributed on a single page numbered 24–25.

If a scene on page 25 were eliminated, a new page 25 would be issued with the word 'OMITTED' written next to the scene number in the scene header. This retires that scene number and it cannot be reused, unless the same scene is reinstated (meaning that the scene has been un-omitted). Again, this is to prevent a mix-up, as having a missing scene or a missing page number would quickly become confusing, and working this way avoids potential errors. It also means that the production company doesn't have to print and distribute an entirely new draft for every set of revisions, and that the crew will not have to transfer their work notes onto an entirely new script every time there are changes.

Scene numbers in a shooting script are handled in a similar way. If scene revisions are made to a shooting script, they must be accomplished in a way that doesn't disturb the pre-existing scene numbers. If a new scene is to be inserted between scenes 10 and 11, the new scene will be numbered 10A. For some productions, it may also be necessary to insert a scene between 10 and 10A – this scene is then numbered 10aA (a scene between 10 and 10aA would be numbered 10aaA and so on). Every scene thus retains its own unique number throughout the course of the production.

To keep scripts orderly, revision pages are distributed on coloured paper, and a different colour is used for each set of revisions. Each change is also notated with an asterisk (*) in the right margin to make them easier to spot. Using coloured pages and asterisks helps to ensure that everyone can see at a glance that the revisions have been circulated and that they are working from the same script with the most up-to-date changes. Changes can affect any element in a script: character, dialogue, locations, day/night, props, action and anything else. This streamlines the process. If more than ten asterisks are needed on a page, they are replaced by a single asterisk in the top corner, which designates 'substantial changes'.

The sequence of page colours varies from one production to the next, but a typical order would be: white, blue, pink, yellow, green, goldenrod, buff, salmon, cherry, tan, ivory, and then back to white (this time known as 'double white'), back to blue ('double blue'), etc.

On occasion, when the assistant director and script editor believe there are more changed pages than are worth swapping out, they may decide to issue an entirely fresh script in the appropriate revision colour. Also, at the start of principal photography, an entirely new 'white draft' will be distributed incorporating all of the revision pages. This is done to start the shooting off with a fresh script; the new white draft will have new page numbers, but the original scene numbers must always be maintained.

If not organised correctly, confusion with scene or page numbering can cause big problems for the entire crew and the production. Cast might not be called at the correct time or on the correct day, sets might not be ready, costume and hair departments might not know what look the cast are meant to have for that scene, props might not be made available; the list of problems is endless when communication breaks down. So it's important that script revisions and formatting be done thoroughly and accurately.

SCRIPT REVISION MEMOS

During shooting on a television production it is common practice for the script editor to also provide what is called a revision memo along with each set of revision pages. This document is used to expedite information and ensure that all departments know and understand how the rewrites have affected the practical and physical needs of the show.

Here is an example of a revision memo. Notice that the revision page colour is listed, as is the revision date. (I also always have the memo printed on the same colour paper as the revisions; this makes it quick to know which revisions are being noted.)

TELEVISION PRODUCTIONS (Company Name)
Series Name – Episode Name
Production office address and contact details would go here...

GREEN REVISION MEMO 16th JUNE 2015 *(Revision colour and date here)*

Episode Three:	*(Episode Number here)*
Page 4, Scene 1E	Trim Mr Hart's first speech. He is now carrying an umbrella.
Page 5, Scene 1F	Internal cut in Dan's first speech.
Page 10	Cut part of scene 14 to blend with scene 13 (13 remains inside the car).
Page 23, Scene 28	Omitted. Blend scene 27 with 29.
Page 28, Scene 40A	Cut the word 'tube', as there is no Wandsworth tube station.
Page 32, 32A, Scene 49	Int. Station – action between Cop and Jean has lengthened. More of a chase now – and Cop has an added line.
Page 37, 37A	Scene 50 is cut.

Page 37, 37A, Scene 51	Simon now enters the station and joins in chase on escalator.
Page 37, 37A, Scene 52	Cop tackles Jean not Simon.
Page 40, Scene 53	Rewritten. This scene no longer takes place in Marty's flat. It now takes place in a wooded area. Amanda is wearing an evening gown and she and Simon dance dreamily.
Page 41, Scene 54	Has been added as we cut back into police station – Cop speaks on the telephone.
Page 41, Scene 52C	Simon no longer drives Jean to the church. It is an unknown driver.

In this memo you can see that the revisions in the script have significantly affected various production departments. In scene 1E, Mr Hart has been given an umbrella – this memo ensures that the prop team will know that an umbrella is now required.

The same types of adjustments happen throughout. Actors added or cut from a scene, for example, might create scheduling issues. In scene 53 the location has changed, as has Amanda's wardrobe. The crew will, of course, also have been given the script revision pages, but this document is an indispensable way of ensuring that the changes will be seen and that elements will not be overlooked.

INTERIOR/EXTERIOR SCENES

Many television shows, particularly serials, have a set number of interior and exterior sets they will use per episode. Exterior sets constitute usually less than 25 per cent of the script, mainly because they are more time-consuming and costly.

Exterior location sets are generally on the studio lot, while interior sets are usually on sound stages. Frequently used sets are predominantly set up permanently, which also saves time. However, there are also reoccurring/floating sets that are used repeatedly, but less frequently, and sometimes an entirely non-studio location will be needed. Locations are a major consideration for any production, but for shows that film multiple episodes weekly this is specifically important. Therefore scripts are written with these considerations up front and it is essential that the writer works within the show's parameters.

Films normally offer more choice and have access to both locations and studio shooting.

CHECKLIST

- Always save a master version of each draft and revision pages of a script; mistakes happen and you may need to go back to an earlier draft or scene. You will want to have every draft easily accessible in your files.

- Make sure all scripts have a header, including date, production title and draft name. And revision colour – on revised pages.

- Make sure pages are printed on appropriate revision colour paper.

- Make sure that pages are locked for the shooting draft and stay locked – and that revisions are placed within the script appropriately. As a courtesy, communicate with the assistant director about when you are locking the pages – make sure that they agree that the production is ready to have them locked. It's your responsibility, but it strongly affects them and it will help if you work as a team.

- Make sure that asterisks are placed alongside any changes in the script.

- Make sure that the OLD asterisks from previous revision changes are removed each time new revisions are made.

- Make sure to include a revision memo with each set of changes.

- Double-check your work – formatting, spelling, page numbers, asterisks – before the changes go out.

SCENE PER PAGE SCRIPT

During production you may be asked to provide a scene per page script. This simply means that you are being asked to create an alternative version of the script that will allow more space for the crew and heads of department to make their notes. To create the scene per page script all you need to do is insert a page break between each and every scene. This version will obviously not have the same page numbers as the official script – that is understood. This version is simply used for notes and the alternate page numbers do not matter.

JOINING THE TEAM OF A LONG-RUNNING SHOW

Working on long-running shows is hard work; it is always very busy, usually very challenging and the hours are extremely long. It can be extremely stressful – but it is a fantastic experience and every day is new and interesting, plus you will learn so much. If you have the chance to join a show, it's a gift and I do recommend you experience it – at least once.

Each show has distinctive requirements in terms of how they organise their production needs. A new script editor joining a long-running show must quickly learn how it operates and work within the pre-existing systems. It's not advantageous for a new team member to come in and try to change the way things work. Over time suggestions may (and probably will) be welcomed – but that comes with trust. As a new member of the team, stick with the procedures that the show has been using. After you have established roots with the show, if there are still ways in which methods can be improved, make your suggestions then. You may find that your first impressions weren't accurate and that suggestions you might have made would not really have worked as well as you once believed. Well-established shows are successful for a reason – they have their working systems in place and have figured out how to keep things running smoothly. So, be patient and work within the system unless something is truly not working – but be certain you have something substantial or effective to offer.

Writing for film requires thinking visually – writing for television is more about the characters and their dialogue.

MORE ABOUT SCRIPT EDITING FILMS

Script editing for films requires all of the skills we've discussed; however, there are variations in how the process flows. Films are able to take more time in both development and production, so the pace can be more forgiving. Still, there may be deadlines and, certainly, once you start shooting, any rewrites will have to be made rapidly. With films, you are working on one long story as opposed to an ongoing series of stories, and unless you are working on a sequel, it's not usually necessary to relate the story or characters to past events or storylines.

In film you will be working with a smaller team of people and there will usually be fewer voices and opinions to navigate among. That doesn't necessarily make it easier, because films are typically much more expensive to make and the pressure to get it right can be even greater.

The biggest difference from a story point of view between movies and TV is that in movies the audience wants the characters to change, but in television the audience wants the characters to stay the same.

In film, audiences want a character arc; they need the character to change, to learn something, to reach a conclusion, a resolution, and to transform in some way. In TV, audiences tend to want the characters to stay the same, to keep struggling from episode to episode and season to season. This, too, seems to be evolving with newer shows, but to a large degree it has stayed the same.

DEVELOPING A SCRIPT WITH A WRITER FROM ITS INCEPTION

It's important in film that something about the story or production offers up some uniqueness. A new world to explore, a new way of telling a story, an extraordinary character; it can be something small, but there has to be a freshness, a new spin, to make it worth doing. Helping writers find that unique element will greatly help them in getting their script made.

Here's a sample of one way I might go about the process:

- The writer comes in with their idea, or various ideas, and we discuss them.

- After a creative discussion, the idea that has generated the most enthusiasm from the writer is the one I suggest we go with, unless it's too similar to another film or overly problematic for some reason.

- The writer then goes away and writes up a short outline or synopsis. They send that to me and we then discuss it again. I give them feedback, ask questions and we discuss how the story can be improved. The writer then reworks the outline and uses that as a platform to go on to the next stage. (If there are a few ideas being considered, this is when I will ask them to decide which one they are most excited about.) If they are having a difficult time deciding, I will ask them to write a premise line to help them figure out which idea is forming better.

- The writer then writes a more in-depth treatment for that outline. I will then give them feedback and we will go into greater detail about the various components of the idea. This is where plot issues tend to show up. At this point there is very little, if any, dialogue or characterisation. Treatments tend to show characters broadly.

- The writer will then either do another pass on the treatment, or they will go to the first draft. I will again suggest that they write or revise their premise line to ensure they are clear about the shape of the story. Once they turn in their first draft, I will give notes. A first draft is still very rough so my notes will be about the bigger issues, such as plot points, conflict, clarity of character motivation – that kind of thing. The writer will then go on to the next draft.

- The process continues in this way. After each draft I will give notes and, once the big elements are in place, we will work on rewrites that focus on whatever specific areas the writer and I deem in need of revision. Often a writer will have a preference as to how they progress through the drafts – typically, plot and structure first, followed by character, followed by dialogue. I will make sure that for each draft the writer is clear about what they are hoping to achieve, and that they set out with specific goals. We will continue working this way until the script is ready.

- Once the script is ready – notice I say 'ready', not 'finished', because it will continue to evolve as time goes on – I will help the writer review the formatting and final polish of the script, ensuring that everything looks professional and is spelt and formatted correctly.

- Then we will work on development documents, submission letters, etc. as needed.

- Once the script has been submitted and read, we wait for feedback. If anything comes out of that feedback that inspires further adjustments, we will address those issues. The process continues until the script has been green-lit. Once green-lit, there may be additional changes to be made, and I may or may not still be working with the writer on the film – that usually depends on the producers. If I am still involved, I will then proceed to coordinate the producer's notes with the writer until the script is ready for production.

- Once in production, script rewrites are still generated by the script editor, but there is now a script supervisor working closely with the script on set. The script supervisor will call up the script editor if any changes are needed or requested, and those will need to be approved by the writer or producer, and in some cases both. These requests can come from various sources: the director might want to adjust something, a production head might discover that something is incorrect, an actor may want a line adjusted, or any amount of other reasons.

- If the changes are small they can be handwritten into the script and the script editor will not issue new pages. If they are bigger, new pages with a new revision colour will be issued. The script editor will give a master copy to the script coordinator and they will run the changes off and have them distributed as needed.

'In comedy laughter settles all arguments.' – Robert McKee

COMEDY TELEVISION

Comedy shows operate differently depending on whether there is a live audience or not.

Single-camera shows, which generally do not have an audience, operate more like mini films than serial television shows or soaps. Again, this can vary – but the principles of how they work are the same, with the important distinction that they need to be funny!

Sitcoms (situation comedy) work a bit differently because they have a live audience.

The situation comedy has proved one of the most enduring and defining genres in television. Sitcoms evoke a unique relationship with their audience, one requiring time to develop an understanding of the characters, the locale, and the humour surfacing from them. Humour stemming from a consistent situation seems a simple concept, but is in fact a complicated form with its own distinctive parameters.

To complicate things further, the UK and US have different ways of working – although in the past few years those lines are getting more blurred, and some UK shows have gravitated towards US methods. The difference between the two styles is that in the US there is a large group of writers working together in 'the writers' room' (numbers range from 12–25) and the show is run by a showrunner.

The showrunner oversees all of the storylines; the group writes as a team to get each of the episodes ready, divvying up the work and rotating who will get credit. Sometimes writers are hired specifically for their strength in one aspect of writing or another, such as story or dialogue, but mostly for adding humour and punching up the jokes.

In the US the title of script editor is not that common, although it is becoming increasingly so. Story editors, script supervisors, script coordinators and writers' assistants do various aspects of the job to a greater or lesser degree, depending on how the showrunner likes to function.

If the script is funny – almost nothing else matters.

COMEDY SCRIPT EDITING

As with all forms, when working with comedic material, the more you understand the mechanics the better, so do your research and get comfortable with how comedy works. To get you started, here is an overall view:

Reading a comedy script

- Always read a comedy script at least twice.

- During your first time reading it through, try to visualise each beat and notate where you laughed.

- Read it the first time without stopping, to get a sense of the flow. This will show you where you are bored, confused, or if you've stopped laughing.

- Notating the laughs helps keep track of where you thought it was funny – and of your first reactions. This is important to do before analysing the humour.

On the second read through make detailed notes and ask the following questions:

- Are the characters working?

- Are there enough jokes?

- Note where there are no laughs and ask why you stopped laughing in that specific area?

- Is the plot set up clearly? Is the dialogue strong enough?

- Is there enough for the central character to do?

- Has the central character disappeared for too long a time in the script?

- Have the characters got enough of a range of emotion in the plot? Meaning, is the plot giving them the opportunity to have significant ups and downs or are they too similar throughout, causing repetition?

- Are the central characters doing enough or are they simply reacting to events?

- Are they having to make some key decisions?

- Are the characters big and comic enough?

- Are they bigger than life but relatable from life?

- Do they have a fatal flaw, comically magnified?

- Is there a sudden leap in the plot, or are the characters behaving unbelievably or inconsistently?

- Do the characters have comic energy?

- Are the characters being introduced with a signature joke?

- Are the plots working? Or are you getting bored with them?

- If you are bored, is that because the main plot is not strong enough? Should the main plot be shifted to a secondary plot (B plot) because it is being stretched too far and is too weak?

- Can the plot matter more – increase in intensity?

- If there isn't enough plot and the story runs out of steam halfway through then maybe it needs to develop more? Or maybe the script needs a subplot or a better subplot that can support the main plot?

- Does the plot need to start earlier?

- Is there enough variety in the plot? If the main plot is downbeat, maybe it needs an upbeat subplot for variety?

- Do some of the characters not have a plot? It's always useful to give all the characters a plot, however small, because that gives them purpose and something to talk about within a scene.

- If the plot doesn't have enough comic set pieces and doesn't build to any sort of ending or resolution, can one be created from things that have happened earlier?

- Is the script making the most of its comic ideas?

> *Just as with all other aspects of script editing, the key to comedy-script editing is asking the right questions:*

- Is the script funny?

- If it isn't funny, WHY isn't it funny?

- What will help make it funnier?

- Is the writer funny?

- If so, why isn't what they're doing funny now?

- Is the basic idea too thin?

- Are the relationships funny enough? (Are there affections, disaffections and rivalries keeping the relationships active and interesting – and funny?)

- Is there a proper sense of hierarchy in terms of job, character and personality?

- Do the characters have key funny characteristics?

- Do the characters belong in the same sitcom?

- Are the episodes taking the characters away from the main setting or relationships and causing a lack of focus?

- Are there too many characters? Are they all needed?

- Do the plots belong in the same sitcom?

- Does each scene have a comic angle and attitude?

- Is the episode being dominated by a guest or minor character too much?

- Is the story believable on its own terms?

- Is the format clear and working properly?

None of these things matter – IF IT'S FUNNY!

- If the script isn't funny, what will help?

Usually by examining these points with the writer you'll be able to help them find ways of making the script funnier – or else, determine why the format isn't working and help the writer move on to another one.

COMEDY NOTES

- As with all note giving, it is wise to start a note session with a positive note. Find something you like about the script and start there.

- As a rule, frame all of your notes in a positive way. 'This is a fantastic idea, there's a potential set piece here – can you get any more jokes out of it?'

- Don't be scared to say 'I don't get this joke'. If you don't get a joke or reference, it's possible that the audience might not either.

- Don't be scared to say 'This isn't funny'. We often skirt around the most important thing that needs saying. In comedy especially, producers and script editors are sometimes embarrassed to tell a writer something isn't funny because it seems a criticism of the very essence of their professionalism. But the truth is that sometimes it just isn't funny and you've got to say so. We all have off days and being told the truth just gives us a chance to make it funny. Also, it's a quick way of learning if this is a writer you can work with. If you can't communicate openly, it's not a good match.

- Don't be scared of sounding stupid. Comedy, in particular, involves tossing around ideas and often you'll have to ask silly and off-the-wall questions. Don't be afraid! If the writer dismisses a question – there's no harm done and it might just lead to the next one that helps the writer get the script into shape. It's comedy! Laugh and have fun with it.

- By asking questions – however silly – you're helping the writer eliminate directions not worth going in.

- Make sure you're not sending the writer in the wrong direction. This can be tricky and you may only find out you've gone horribly wrong with experience. But one way to avoid going too far off track is by encouraging the writer to take time to sleep on an idea. It's easy to get carried away with an idea in a meeting. So, it's worth considering and then coming back with fresh eyes, to see if it still seems like it works after greater consideration.

- Remember it's not your sitcom; it's the writer's. They will have to spend months writing it – so don't impose your sitcom on them.

- On the other hand, be prepared to argue if you think they're going down the wrong path. And argue as persuasively (and respectfully) as you can.

HOW A JOKE WORKS

- Familiarity. By using familiar topics such as religion, family and office dynamics, sex – and doing routines on them.

- Contrast. By using juxtaposition of opposites. Consider the worst boss in the world (such as David Brent from *The Office*), juxtaposed with his nemesis, Neil Godwin, who is characterised as the best boss in the world.

- Surprise. By using surprise – getting the audience to think the story is going in one direction, but then providing a twist at the end. Lots of comedy is about sending the audience the wrong way. Try to find dialogue that offers ambiguity.

- Anticipation. By leaving a gap for the audience to fill in, or by making them wait for the joke. If the audience is complicit in the joke because they've worked out the double entendre, or have to work to 'get it', they feel self-satisfaction and laugh all the more.

- Rule of three. By using the rule of three – a writing principle that suggests that things that come in threes are inherently funnier, more satisfying, or more effective than other numbers of things.

- Redirecting. By creating a pattern and then switching it up or having it blow up.

- Verbal repartee and banter. By using wordplay. Lots of comedy is about wordplay. Look for ambiguities in sound and meaning.

- Inventiveness. By using lateral thinking – a comic leap of imagination. Comedy is about inventing comic scenarios.

- Technique. By using comedy techniques such as: exaggeration, comic juxtaposition, twisting the familiar, the gap, surprise through ambiguity, sending the audience the wrong way, rule of three, comic observation, visual jokes.

COMEDY FORMAT

- What is the script/show really about?

- How is it relatable? (For example, *Steptoe and Son* isn't just about rag and bone men – it's about parents and children. *Till Death Us Do Part* isn't just about family, but also working-class life and exploring racial and political issues.

- What are the centres of action? Keep to two or three, but pick the best ones.

- The more characters there are, the fewer the centres of action. (For example, in *Dad's Army* they're all in the hall. We don't follow them home so the focus is simple.)

COMEDY CHARACTERS

- Are the characters archetypes or clichés?

- Are the characters bigger than life but still recognisable and authentic? (Basil Fawlty, for example, is much bigger than life and his extreme behaviour, although outrageous, is recognisable. Take the episode 'Gourmet Night' – we appreciate Basil's frustration at his car breaking down and laugh as he beats it because we've all felt that kind of anger; however, most of us don't go to his lengths in expressing it.)

- Is the writer showing not telling? Remind them to reveal character through action.

- Are they avoiding plain backstory and exposition? Encourage writers to give their characters an attitude to what they're telling us or are being told.

- What are the key relationships? Sitcoms are about relationships as much as about characters and situations.

- Do the central characters' relationships bring out different aspects of their personalities? The simplest way to achieve this is by putting them in some form of hierarchy (such as Basil Fawlty, who is subservient with his wife Sybil, but a cruel tyrant boss with Manuel).

COMEDY PLOT

- Life should get increasingly problematic for the characters, and just when they think they've solved the problem... it should get even worse. If writers go too easy on their characters, it dilutes the comedy.

- What are the central characters doing?

- Have they got a story?

- Are they initiating their problems and making them worse and/or solving them?

- Is the story letting them go through a range of emotions?

- Does the story take them from triumph to despair – and back again? Humour comes from the extreme.

THE COMEDY

- Are the characters and relationships funny?

- Do the characters have a signature joke or characteristic?

- Are the plots enabling the characters to be funny? Are they offering opportunities for inappropriate behaviour? (Examples include *The Office*, *Alan Partridge*, *Da Ali G Show*.)

- Does each scene have a comic angle and attitude?

Comedy writing is an art unto itself – and one that I hold in extremely high regard. I've been lucky to work on some really funny scripts with terrific writers. Working in comedy is a great existence, and shooting in front of a live audience is the cherry on top. It's exciting to see a script come to life in front of an audience. The roar of laughter is addictive – and who wouldn't love to earn a living laughing all day? I highly recommend it.

REWRITES

*It takes time to find a story, and even more time
to make it really work.*

After the notes on the current draft have been analysed and discussed, rewrites are inevitable. How you guide the writer as to which way to proceed varies depending on the parameters of the project, but the most important first step is to have an agreed plan of action. The biggest problem with most rewrites is that the writer will typically start on page one and just work their way through, tweaking as they go, moving commas and not really focusing on what specifically they are doing. It's very easy for writers to get waylaid by the notes they've been given or by their desire to trim or clean the script up without having a specific goal in mind, and they can too easily end up rewriting things that are actually working fine, while neglecting areas with problems.

Therefore, before starting a rewrite it is important they are focused on the direction they need to take. The best way forward is to decide on specific goals and rework with that in mind. In order to help writers organise those goals, here is a checklist as a reminder of what to be looking for.

- **Concept/premise line:** review the script with an eye to making sure the overall concept works. Remember that the premise line is an abbreviated version of the script and if it isn't clear and working efficiently then the writer needs to start the rewrite by rethinking what the core of the story is. (The logline is the most abbreviated version of the script – and hopefully the writer will have a logline written as well.)

- **Genre:** review the framework of the genre of the intended story and make sure it is working. If it's a comedy, is it making you laugh? If it's a drama, is it making you cry? This may sound extreme, but if it's not moving at this stage, it won't be moving on film.

- **Story:** is the story clear? Are the first ten pages strong and do they hook the reader? Does the story have a beginning, middle and end? Is the plot giving the characters enough conflict or is the writer being too easy on them? Are the stakes high enough?

- **Characters:** who is the protagonist? Is it clear? Does the protagonist have enough flaws? Are they strong enough to support the plot? Are they interesting people? Do the character descriptions/ essence statements offer us a strong but concise look into the characters? Are there strong first meets (meaning the first time we meet the characters)? Do they make a strong impression?

- **Dialogue:** is the dialogue natural-sounding? Is there enough subtext or is the dialogue too on the nose? Is the writer showing and not telling throughout? Is the exposition sufficiently concealed?

- **Pacing:** does the story have momentum? Does the pace vary? Are there peaks and low points?

- **Scenes:** do scenes flow smoothly? Do they end with a question or problem to be worked out? Does each scene turn? Are the scenes focused and about the characters in it?

- **Theme:** is it clear that the writer has something to say with this story? Does the story clearly express the theme? Are there lessons learned?

- **Voice and originality:** does the writer have an original voice? Is the idea and execution of the story original? Are there surprises?

- **Formatting:** is the formatting consistent? Are the names and locations listed consistently? Are the pages numbered? Are the action lines concise and clearly telling us what the characters are doing? Are the pages visual, but not cluttered with camera directions? Has the writer proofed for typos and grammatical errors? (This comes into play during later drafts.)

With this list in mind, decide (and discuss with the writer) which of these areas need work and what you want to accomplish with each rewrite. Have the writer focus on only those specific elements with each pass, looking at the story from only those specific points of view. For example, if you want to strengthen a relationship between two characters, have the writer focus only on those two characters during the rewrite, allowing them time to find new ways to support the characters and rework scenes that support those objectives.

CONCENTRATED NOTES

If a script has major structural or story problems, it really isn't constructive to give all of your notes to the writer – it will only overwhelm and potentially discourage them. In these instances, it's much better to give them the one or two essential notes that will help get the story on track. There is no point fixing smaller details, such as dialogue, etc., if there are bigger problems to face. So, prioritise. This can seem difficult, especially if you are working with a newer writer who wants to hear all of your thoughts about the script, but understand that it will only distract them from the real issues at hand. Sort those out first, and then see where you are. The script may change significantly and issues you had at the beginning of the process might be sorted out naturally without your commenting on them.

SCRIPT EDITOR AS LIAISON

There may be numerous people the writer is getting feedback from, especially if production is about to commence, or is underway. A script editor's job is to help the screenwriter with this process. If there are multiple executives and creative personnel involved, then the task becomes more complicated. The more voices and opinions thrown at the writer, the harder it is for them to decipher which notes are going to propel the story towards the desired goal. This is why notes should be channelled through the script editor, who will condense them, prioritise them and communicate them to the writer in an understandable and acceptable way, while guiding them forward. However, sometimes notes come from other directions with seemingly good intentions. It's at those times that diplomacy is crucial.

Those paying for the script and development of a project have a lot at stake and will often be very involved in how material evolves. This is understandable, but it's important that the script editor protect the writer from confusing or conflicting notes, meandering ideas that are not clear or specific, and negative or unhelpful comments that might upset or delay the process. The script editor is there to act as a liaison – to ensure that the producer's notes are being put forth and facilitated, but also that the writer's ideas and work are being respected. Again, in a perfect world the writer and producers will all be on the exact same page and the way forward will be very clear. BUT this is not always the case! On occasion, I've seen enormous differences between what a producer thinks they have commissioned and what a writer believes is expected of them.

I was recently brought in on a project which was a historical drama. The young, up-and-coming writer-director hired me to assess their script. He was pulling his hair out because he couldn't find a way to make the notes that his producers were giving him work. I read the script and then read through the pile of notes. It became obvious very quickly that the producers thought they were making a comedy, while the writer-director was intending to make a historical drama. I was astonished that the company had got to the second draft and had not realised this most basic fact themselves, but these misunderstandings happen all the time. It's vital that communication between the writer and producers is crystal clear, otherwise a project can be in rewrites for ages, causing a great deal of frustration – or worse, resulting in a good project being shelved. Even more upsetting is when the writer is held accountable for the miscommunication and replaced.

This type of confusion would be highly unlikely to happen if a script editor was employed on the project. Getting everyone on the same page from the very beginning is essential. A script editor would have immediately seen that the two parties were coming from different points of view and were making two very different kinds of film. They would have coordinated conversations to address this issue up front, instead of allowing six months and two drafts to pass by before figuring out that there were fundamental discrepancies. This was an extreme case, but these kinds of problems are far too common. A script editor will prevent such difficulties occurring, saving time and money by ensuring that there is consensus around a project.

Notes to the writer should be given in a clear, positive and concise way that reflect specific goals, without meandering thoughts that aren't relevant or specific. Writing and rewriting is hard enough, and if there are a variety of people giving notes, there will be varied versions and interpretations of what is expected. Even if all the people involved have the same intentions, things easily become confused. That is just the nature of communication, and having one spokesperson, whose job it is to make sure that the notes and directions are clearly understood, simply makes sense. Having that one person be a script editor, someone who knows how to work with content, writers and producers and work to a deadline, is a very practical and beneficial solution.

INTERPRETING NOTES – THE NOTE UNDER THE NOTE

Deadlines can be harsh and often the executive producer, producers, series editor, etc., don't have time to copiously analyse the script or script revisions to a great extent. They read a draft and their notes tend to be 'gut reactions' – educated and instinctive, rather than fully formed or thought through. A script editor must interpret their notes correctly, trying to get to the bottom of what they really mean, and getting to the heart of what the note is really about.

For example, a note might be that the protagonist does something in a scene that the producer finds unrealistic for that character. It's not very helpful to give a note to the writer that suggests something isn't realistic or believable, because they have (or should have) already considered why the character is behaving in that way when they wrote the draft. Instead, it's more useful to find out why the producer didn't engage with the character in that scene. What was it about the scene that struck a negative chord? Not being likable or believable usually has something to do with not being able to engage with the character at that point.

Another example is if the producer says something incredibly vague – that the first half of a scene doesn't work, for instance, and they were bored. Again, that's not a note you want to pass on to the writer. It will only create bad feelings. The script editor's job is to figure out why it didn't work, and what made it boring, and to express that to the writer in a way they will understand. In this scenario, it may be that the scene is too similar to another in the script; maybe the scene is focusing on a character we don't really know well or care about yet; maybe it's too long and needs trimming. These are the kinds of notes a writer can work with. So, having identified the specific problem, you are in a better position to communicate what isn't working and help the writer find solutions.

> *Finding the 'note under the note' means finding*
> *the root cause of the note.*

Another scenario is that sometimes a producer will offer up what they consider a great 'fix' to a problem. Unfortunately, these fixes are seldom something the writer really wants to do, so the script editor must then work between the two to come up with a cheerful solution. It's also the script editor's job to figure out what other problems the 'fix' might generate, and help writers come up with their own solutions. That solution might not even be close to what the producer had in mind, but usually, if it solves the problem, everyone will be happy. Of course, there are times when the producer or director is adamant that their fix is the best or only way things will work, and you must then take a deep breath and organise your thoughts very clearly – don't play the two parties against each other, but work gently to untangle the situation until everyone agrees (or at least makes a decision) that solves the problem. During this dance, diplomacy and poise are your best friends.

SCRIPT EDITOR – THE VOICE OF REASON AND LOGIC

During rewrites there are often times when research and fact checking are necessary. Often the script editor will help with that. It's really important that material be authentic, particularly in historical and biographical stories. As I have mentioned before, maintaining story logic is crucial. The script editor will usually be the first person to question the authenticity and logic of the script's story elements. Of course, filmmakers manipulate the truth for filmic purposes constantly, but the core facts must be identified before those artistic choices can be made. The script editor will often be the 'voice of reason' – or the 'logic police', as some have called it. They will double-check particulars to ensure that locations, periods, real people and situations are being depicted correctly. And they will constantly ask logical questions. It's not always easy being the person asking these kinds of practical questions, but it has to be done. They will come up eventually! It's better that they are faced head on, rather than trying to piecemeal a solution together later. At the end of the day, it's all done with the intention of making the script the best it can be – and doing so with as little stress as possible, and with care and respect.

THE TIME KEEPER

Commissioned projects have pros and cons – the pros are that the writer is aware of their obligation to the project and to the collaborative nature of what they are doing. The cons are that the writer and script editor have to come up with the script, and are less able to walk away from a project that isn't working or to their liking. In television, especially, the pace is fast. Not all writers can produce rewrites at the speed necessary for production, and usually production dates are inflexible, so deadlines are firm. If a writer and script editor aren't getting the job done in a timely fashion, there is pressure on everyone, and it's very possible that the producer will decide that replacements are necessary.

It is the script editor's responsibility to ensure that a writer gets their project in on deadline. That can be difficult because, as much as you can aid with that, it's also very much out of your control. All you can really do is gently (or aggressively, depending on what is needed) stay in contact with the writer, know what is going on and where they are within the framework of the goals set up, and help them find solutions when there are difficulties.

Sometimes difficulties come in the form of personal problems. Script editors must be good listeners. Try to help where you can. Of course, you are not a therapist, but you can be a springboard, a resource, and potentially a friend. Always remember, though, to keep the business of finishing the script your central focus. Speak frankly when there are difficulties and keep everyone who needs to be informed of how things are going.

Again, remember to set realistic deadlines within the framework of the project, and express your concerns if these aren't being met. Help the writer stay on target by checking in regularly – via email, phone, Skype, or however you agree to do it. Don't invade their writing time or hound them with too many disturbances, but sort out a method that you agree on and stay in touch. Be consistent.

PAGE COUNT

One of the regular challenges for a writer is keeping the script to a decent page count. Condensing an idea into a concise, extremely well-organised and entertaining script takes a while. Early drafts tend to be too long, and they seem to get longer before they can get shorter. Composing material takes time and work, and it's important that the writer feel unconstrained in the early stages of the journey. This is a process, and the writer must have the freedom and space to develop the story without too many limitations. Don't worry about page count during the early drafts. Yes, it will need to be trimmed. Yes, it might mean cutting some things that are loved. But it will also allow for the best of the material to be selected and for the concepts and ideas of the story to flourish.

Eventually, the script will have to come in at a reasonable page count, and if the script you are editing is very long, you will have to review with the writer, in the way that feels most comfortable to them, each scene with these questions in mind:

- Make sure each scene has significance. Go scene by scene and ask, 'Does this scene contain relevant information?'

- Does the scene simultaneously develop character?

- Does the scene illuminate the themes of the film?

- Is it important to keep the scene in the script? Is it necessary?

- Does the page look well organised and balanced? Or is the writing dense and difficult on the eye? Too much black ink in a script (dense dialogue and description) can make the reading of it drag. Try to convince the writer to trim overly crowded pages down. The easier a page is on the eyes, the more likely it is that a reader will enjoy it.

- Does the scene start at the latest possible moment? Or is there too much backstory and introduction taking up space and slowing the story down?

- Does the scene end at the best possible point, giving it completion but also ending early enough so that the next scene flows effectively?

- Is the scene entertaining? Is it cinematic, visual, or is it just functional? Actors call functional scenes 'laying the pipe', meaning they contain information the audience needs, but that the scene itself isn't very interesting. Try to help the writer find a way to get that information across in a more unique and exciting way. Perhaps by introducing it in another scene, or by blending, weaving, reorganising or redistributing scenes or dialogue? Look for a visual way of revealing the information. In any case, finding distinctive ways to divulge exposition is essential.

Each scene should hold its own and stand out, be effective, provide new information, have purpose, and move the story forward. Scene craft is an art. It takes time and experience to get it right.

THE NEXT STEP

Once it has been established that all the scenes are in order, make logical sense, progress well and are absolutely necessary, it's time to go page by page through the script.

The writer should read through all of the descriptions and action lines, trimming back anything that is superfluous. If there is a description that is three sentences long, try to get it down to one or two.

'If the character raises her cup of coffee to her lips,
that's not important enough to describe… unless there's
poison in the cup.' – David Trottier

The writer should also review all the dialogue, making sure that there is little excess. That is not to say that they should lose characterisation, development or important dialogue. Obviously, the cadence of speech for a character is vital to their persona. Don't try to get the writer to trim so much that all the characters sound similar. But do have them cut where and when it feels overwritten, unnecessary, or in particular where information is repeated.

Repeating information is a common mistake newer writers
make. Point those areas out and help them understand where
emphasis is needed, and where it becomes redundant.

At the end of the day, content and flavour are important, but so is brevity. Helping the writer find that balance is a key part of the job. After multiple drafts, or when nearing a deadline, it may be that you have to ask the writer to be ruthless with their cutting. This can be very distressing for the writer, especially if you are asking for 10, 15 or 20 pages of cuts! However, once done, it usually makes for a much tighter, more powerful script. Plus it means that the director or producers won't be deciding on those cuts for the writer – or filming costly extra scenes that will end up on the cutting room floor. It serves the writer to make those choices themselves ahead of time.

There are times, however, when a few extra pages can make all the difference – in a positive way. The world of storytelling is an intricate dance, and there are exceptions to every rule. So, keeping an open mind is essential.

Sadly, I know of readers who will check the page count of a script and simply not bother to read a submission if it's too long. I disapprove of that attitude, and will always give the writer a chance. Some of the most beloved films of all time would be considered too long today. I will not reject a project simply due to its length, but a story must be worthy of it. Remember, it's all about finding the best way to tell the story, and sometimes it takes a few more pages for the script to pay off. More often than not, however, a few less would be better.

COMMON SCRIPT PROBLEMS

SOFT SCRIPTS

A 'soft script' refers to a script that has too little tension, weak character arcs and a vague or insipid premise. A soft script generally stems from there not being enough going on within the story. Soft scripts are one of the most common problems with screenplays, especially for newer writers.

Storytelling is about conflict and in a soft script there just isn't enough conflict to keep it interesting. Again, the amount and kind of conflict varies, depending on the genre of the script and it's important that the writer adheres to the rules of the genre in order to satisfy the audience.

New writers tend to write very autobiographical and personal scripts. These can be the best scripts, with the most authentic voices and unique situations. After all, the saying 'Write what you know' is proposing just that. But it's not an easy thing to accomplish. Writing close to home can prove very difficult – it takes tremendous objectivity, and when it comes to our pasts, to our families, our friends, or to ourselves, it's hard to be objective. Without objectivity it's hard to create a well-rounded story. It can also be tremendously challenging for a writer to deviate from what they feel 'really happened' in order to satisfy the needs of the script, or be brutally honest with characters based on people with whom they have relationships. Such obstacles cause subjectivity, and often make ultra-personal scripts imbalanced or uninteresting. In those cases, it's highly important that the writer take a long, hard and honest look at the story they are telling and make certain it offers enough universal interest and truth to engage an audience – and that they are in a frame of mind to write it boldly and without restraint.

OVERLY COMPLICATED AND UNFOCUSED SCRIPTS

Writers can get lost in minuscule details or create convoluted story concepts and lose sight of the central story idea – or even neglect to have one. In these scripts, there will tend to be long and wordy descriptions, excessively dense action lines, and way too much exposition resulting in a draft that is confusing overall.

In these cases, the script editor should steer the writer back to the beginning of the process, asking the basic story questions to help them streamline the story and obtain control over the script.

INCOMPLETE SCRIPTS

Sometimes writers will write themselves into a corner and not know how to proceed. If you are working with a writer who is stuck, the same process applies – guide them back to the basic story questions and root them back into the heart of what they are trying to accomplish.

If the writer is unsure of the story they are telling, then they must take the time to re-evaluate what they are doing and find their motivation and purpose. A script editor can be a great sounding board, and will hopefully help the writer to rekindle their passion for what they have started.

KNOWING WHEN IT IS DONE

Once the problems are solved – the script flows well, the characters are rich and vibrant, the relationships are working, the dialogue is strong, and the story is satisfying – it's time to leave the script alone. So, stop editing! Let the project breathe. Things may need a small tweak here or there during shooting, but for now, just enjoy the fact that the script you have worked on for so very long is now in good shape.

It's very easy for a writer to spend an interminable amount of time doing revisions. So, it really helps if there is a plan of action. It's a script editor's job to help the writer focus on specific tasks in the work, and try to prevent them from obsessively tweaking things that don't really matter.

To help with this make sure the writer:

- Is organised and has a plan of action.

- Is reminded not to waste time by altering things without a plan, but to collect their thoughts and work with a goal in mind.

- Remembers to stick closely to the script outline/treatment/notes they are using and stay focused on the story they are telling.

- Takes a break when needed. Sometimes a break is the best way to get clarity! Occasionally the writer just needs a breather from the work and should take a few days (or weeks?) to let their thoughts settle. A break will usually allow them to return to the project with fresh eyes and enthusiasm for the work.

IN EXTREME CASES...

There are times when writers get so frustrated that they consider throwing out an entire script and starting all over again. This is seldom wise; better to refine through redrafting than to discard a large amount of work. Time is precious and chances are the writer will end up with much of the same material.

Remember, there are all kinds of writers. Some are great ideas people, who put out solid and promising first drafts, but aren't great at reworking or finessing them. Other writers work slower, their scripts improving with each draft as they find the voice that suits the story and the characters. But the truth is, it is the writers able to do rewrites who are usually the most successful in the business, because it is such an essential part of the development process. Unless writers are financing the project themselves, the story will have to advance into a script that excites a producer enough to generate funding to have it made. A good script editor can greatly assist writers through this process, by helping them to identify the story problems and steering them towards positive solutions – ensuring that they don't 'band aid' over story weaknesses that will only come back to further trouble them.

Even if rewriting doesn't come naturally, if a writer really wants to be successful, it is a skill that they'll need to acquire.

FORMATTING INFORMATION AND TECHNICAL ISSUES

Reading scripts is a fantastic way to gain understanding of how screenplays are constructed. Read as many as you can and take the time to analyse what worked and what didn't. Read all kinds – your favourite films, samples from different genres, films that you feel have failed – and examine the way they have been put together. Try to uncover why they worked and where they were unsuccessful. Go through the lists of questions in this book and see where the scripts are solid and where the elements are unfocused or weak. The more you read, the more you will learn and the clearer the entire process of script assessing will become.

There are free websites with downloadable scripts, which are a great resource for learning script construction. I have included a list of websites offering free scripts in the resources section of this book. BUT be warned: scripts posted on websites are frequently 'shooting' scripts or 'revised' drafts and may not provide the best samples for formatting purposes. Nevertheless, as far as content goes, they are very worthwhile.

SCRIPT FORMATTING

It is very important that writers use the correct formatting for their work. Not only does this give their script a professional appearance, but it also allows the reader to enjoy the writing without undesirable distractions. Having it look and read proficiently goes a long way towards having a producer or reader take the script and the writer seriously.

If a script looks unrefined or slapdash, with typos, etc., it makes a bad impression and gives the appearance that the writer doesn't really care. And frankly, if the writer doesn't care, then why should anyone else? I've known readers to reject a script on page one because it had numerous typos. This may sound harsh but, when your job is to read scripts all day, after a while it becomes very tiring reading those that are not proficient and it gets easier to dismiss them outright.

Do your writers a favour and make sure they learn how to proofread their scripts and format properly.

THE CORRECT FORMAT FOR SCREENPLAYS

• Font – scripts must be written in 12 point Courier typeface or Courier (New) 12 point.

• A4 paper with approximately 55 lines per page. (Regardless of paper size, if in the US simply adjust top and bottom margins accordingly.) 55 lines does not include the page number.

• Left margin – 1.5 inches.

• Right margin – 1 inch (between .5 inches and 1.25 inches).

• 1 inch top and bottom margins.

• The text justified from the left with specific tabs for the different elements and appropriate line spacing.

• Character speaking (dialogue) is listed in all caps, 3.7 inches from the left side of the page (2.2 from the margin).

• Dialogue – 2.5 inches from the left side of the page (1.5 from the margin).

- Number pages on the top-right-hand corner, but do not number the scenes. Numbers should be followed by a period. The title page should not be numbered and it does not count as a page. The first page of the script is also not numbered, but it is page one. The first page to have a number is the second page of the screenplay. (To clarify, this is the third sheet of paper in the script – 1 is the title page; 2 is page one, but is not numbered; 3 is the second page of the script and is numbered page 2.)

- Parentheticals (known as wrylies) are set at 3.1 inches from the left side of the page (1.6 from the margin). Parentheticals are used only to prevent confusion about a line that could be interpreted multiple ways.

  For example, the writer might have a line like this:

  JULIA
  Nice outfit!

  However, this line might not be as straightforward as it appears. Perhaps it's meant as a dig? In order to inform the reader what its proper intention is, a writer might add a parenthetical, like this:

  JULIA
  (sarcastically)
  Nice outfit!

  Writers should use parentheticals sparingly as too many of them slow the pace down and grow tiresome for the readers, the actors and the director. Use them only when it is essential.

- Listing camera angles should also be avoided, as should any directing on the page – that is the director's job and slows down the reading of the script. Writers may suggest what they want by creating an image through the writing – for example, if a writer sets the opening scene of their film on a large farm in Wales with rolling hills and sheep grazing, we will automatically understand that this is going to be a wide shot. No camera angle listing required.

PAGE LAYOUT

- Each scene will have a heading or slug line, written in capitals, 1.5 inches from the left. INT./EXT. is used to designate indoors or outdoors, followed by the location and whether it is day or night, e.g. INT. KITCHEN – DAY.

- Next is the scene description, denoting what the setting is, who the characters are, and what action is going on in the scene. This is double-spaced below the slug line, 1.5 inches from the left. The lines of the scene description should be single-spaced, with ragged rather than justified text and no more than 7.5 inches from the left. REMEMBER to keep the action succinct.

- The first time a character appears, put their name in capitals. If possible, break up the action lines into paragraphs of a maximum of four lines at a time – this makes it easier to read.

- The character's name (also called a cue) should be in capitals, 3.5 inches from the left, with a single return.

- Under the character's name will be the dialogue. Each line of dialogue should be 2.5 inches from the left and no more than 3.5 inches long. Do not hyphenate long words and do not break a sentence from one page to the next. When a character's dialogue goes over the page, write (MORE) next to the character cue and, on the following page, repeat the character cue with (CONT'D) next to it.

- There should be a double space between the dialogue and the next element – be it another character's name, action or new scene heading.

- Action – if there is a line of action within the scene, for example, 'Stan punches him in the stomach', this should be formatted in the same way as the scene description.

- Transitions between scenes such as CUT TO: indicating a sharp cut, or DISSOLVE TO: indicating the passage of time, are written in capitals 5.5 inches from the left. You do not need to use transitions, however, as this is implied by the movement from one scene to another.

The best way to understand all the workings of script format is to read screenplays. Make sure they are in film rather than theatre or a revised format. There are many good books on the topic.

Please note that screenplays sold in book versions will be in various fonts, but that this is a design element specific to the printed version.

Also, be aware that it is not uncommon for A-list auteurs who write, direct, produce and sometimes even edit their own work to include very detailed camera directions with long action blocks and character descriptions in their scripts. These filmmakers are considered independent and are NOT necessarily looking for commercial funding or to be commissioned and so are less concerned about 'industry standards'. This is true of some top-notch filmmakers and they know very clearly what they are doing and can afford to deviate from the norm. Most writers are not in this position and it's considered poor form to assume that place if you haven't earned it. So, until they do, try to convince your writers to work within the suggested guidelines unless they have a REALLY good reason not to.

SOFTWARE

It has become common for writers to use screenwriting software programs to ensure correct formatting. There are a few on the market, but I have always used Final Draft; it's easy to learn and well worth the investment if you are going to be working with screenplays on a regular basis. I am told that some of the other programs are very good, too, but Final Draft is the only one that I have personally used. Most of them will give you a trial period to test them out, so you may as well become familiar with one of them as soon as you can.

PROFESSIONAL **ADVICE**

In the hope of planting fertile seeds for future script editors and writers, I have interviewed some extraordinary talent (writers, producers, script editors) to discuss how they work, how they solve problems that come up, and what they consider important during development. I have incorporated much of their wisdom within the previous chapters and will now offer some remaining thoughts to consider.

WHEN WRITERS AND PRODUCERS DON'T AGREE...

There are times when everyone on a project seems to disagree, and the question of loyalty and integrity on a job becomes a tricky one. During these times, the politics of script editing can be very complicated. It is important to maintain good relationships, and it can be quite daunting trying to remain loyal to the writer, satisfy a producer or producers and safeguard the needs of the project, while also maintaining your own integrity.

When these kinds of situations develop, remind yourself that the script editor is there to support the process.

As a script editor I'm often asked 'Whose side are you on – the producer's or the writer's?' The truth is, in order to do a thorough job you have to be on the writer's side. How else are you going to be able to make a strong connection with them and aid them in the process? You are there as the writer's support system. But the reality is that script editors are usually hired and paid for by the production, not the writer. So you also have a big responsibility to them. The best way to view the situation is that, ultimately, your responsibility is to the project you're working on and making the script the best it can possibly be. So, at the end of the day, you're on the side of the work, which means supporting the writer AND the team putting the project together. It is a collaborative process, after all, and so you must find the right balance.

SPEAKING WITH WRITERS

As with any working relationship, it's important to find a positive way of communicating. Being respectful is fundamental. There is little chance of developing a strong relationship with a writer if the script editor is dismissive, sarcastic, negative, judgemental or unkind. It is also not of any value for the writer to have a script editor who is a sycophant. Honest and constructive criticism is the only way forward.

As a script editor it is essential that you are sincere about your appraisal and that no matter what your judgements are, you are capable of backing them up with reasoned argument and expressing them clearly. Creative individuals are often very sensitive about their work and it is important that you use the correct language when approaching criticism.

Wording issues as questions is often the best way to proceed. For example, if there is a character in the script who you feel is not as developed as they should be, rather than saying, 'The character of so and so is flat and uninteresting,' you might ask the writer what that character's purpose is in the story – and then follow that up by explaining that their purpose wasn't quite clear. Then ask if they would consider giving the character more to do, or ask that they reveal their purpose or motivation in the story to a greater degree.

This approach usually works, but every now and then you will find a writer who insists they want things spelt out more directly – and some will even tell you to be 'brutally honest'. I warn you against ever being brutally honest! People say they want that, but the creative temperament is fragile and being brutal will only lead to distrust and hostility. Truth is, what they want is simply a straightforward and honest approach – and that is a very reasonable request. The key is to get to the heart of the matter, work with the individual sensibilities, but always be constructive.

Help the script to get better, but not at the cost of the writer.

PRIORITISING NOTES

Misunderstandings develop when script editors are unaware of where in the process the writer is coming from. Discuss this with them up front; know what stage the writer is at with their work before diving into making decisive remarks. During early drafts remember not to get overly specific with notes, because at that point it's the intention of the writing that is important. Showing an early draft is a scary proposition for most writers, and it's frustrating for them to be given notes about lesser details when they are occupied with bigger aspects of the story.

On the other hand, it's also important that you not walk around on eggshells. If you think something, say it – ideas come from having in-depth conversations. The more comfortable you become with the writer the easier these conversations will become. You should always speak your mind, but with well thought through comments and examples to back up your opinions. And if the writer doesn't go for the idea – drop it. Find another way into the story. Your job is to spot the problems and help the writer find the solutions.

Truth be told, I have spoken with quite a few script editors who admit that they have, on occasion, helped writers by providing fixes or potential solutions. As I have said repeatedly... this is not your job, but every now and then (and I mean seldom!) it becomes evident that you can, in fact, really help by offering up an idea. It's better to try and steer the writers into finding the answer for themselves, but once in a blue moon – you may decide to break this rule. Don't forget that finding a solution doesn't necessarily mean that the problem is solved. The writers must still find their own way inside any solution to make them work.

WORKING WITH WRITER-DIRECTORS

Working with writer-directors can present unique challenges and the most common one is that they may try to resolve problems by simply moving the camera or incorporating editing techniques. These devices can work to a large degree, but nothing can replace getting the story right. If there are inconsistencies or weaknesses in the story/ premise, it's your job to remind the writer-director that those flaws will probably be detected if not thought through and fixed properly ahead of time. Often writer-directors are stretched very thin time-wise during pre-production and definitely during production. It will be much easier and less stressful if the script is in good shape before then.

WORKING WITH CO-WRITERS AND WRITING TEAMS

When working with co-writers it's important to understand the dynamics of how they work together. Over time you will learn about their strengths and weaknesses, their preferences and the relationship between them, but in the early stages make sure to ask the basics, like what kind of work schedule they keep and where they meet to work; what the specifics of their system are, such as who types, who proofreads, and how they make decisions when they disagree on something.

I've worked with many writing teams and I love it – especially when they have a strong connection. It enhances the work and provides an additional support within the framework. I personally have never had a bad experience working with writing partners, but I am sure there are plenty of cases where one member is easier than the other, or that on occasion communication/relationships between the partners becomes strained. If that happens, all you can do is use your common sense. Try to keep the stress minimised and give the team room to sort out their own differences. It's not unusual to have one writer be the spokesperson, which can really help, but make sure not to neglect the other one, and don't assume they tell each other everything. Make sure to follow up yourself to ensure information has been distributed to all parties, unless otherwise arranged for a specific reason.

GREATER AND LESSER EXPERIENCE

It can be challenging for a seasoned writer to work with a newer script editor and this certainly happens regularly, especially in television. If you find yourself in this position, it's important to recognise and acknowledge the writer's ability and gain their trust right away by being completely prepared and getting on with the work diligently. Don't pretend to know things you don't know – and don't be afraid to ask questions when you need to. Stay calm and listen to what the writer tells you. Don't sit there waiting for them to stop talking so that you can speak – focus on what they are communicating. Better to hold off on your thoughts if they are vague and unformed. It's perfectly acceptable to say you need to take a bit of time to consider an idea they have brought up. At the same time, don't be afraid to be yourself and enjoy the process!

On the flip side, experienced script editors usually embrace working with newer writers because it's exciting to discover new ideas and talent. However, if there is an intense deadline, or if the writer is greatly lacking in craft and/or discipline, this can also be very frustrating. The best remedy is to maintain an open communication. Voice your concerns WHEN necessary and try to help the writer establish a working arrangement that creates productivity.

PROFESSIONAL ETIQUETTE

Get back to writers swiftly about their script. Any longer than a few weeks is rude. If you simply can't get to it before then, at least get in touch and let them know. When a writer sends a script they are eager to know what you think. Be considerate and don't keep them waiting too long.

After all, without writers you have no job, so you need to nurture them and create good relationships.

If they're commissioned, they're working to a deadline, so there's even more reason to get back to them. They probably need a quick response so they know they're going in the right direction.

Give proper, specific notes. Really read the script. Writers can tell if you haven't read the work properly – they're usually just too polite to say so. Or too concerned about offending a person who might help give them work. Even if the script is terrible, get back to the writer in a timely and productive fashion. It's only good manners.

THE SCRIPT IS DONE – NOW WHAT?

There are different points of view regarding how involved a script editor should become with a project after the script has been completed. For some the job ends there, but others stay on board, introducing projects to producers and broadcasters, etc. Many even produce projects in their own right. It is certainly a natural progression for a script editor or development executive to go on to produce. The parameters really depend on the temperament of the script editor and what they are interested in accomplishing.

Producing is very much about sales and not everyone is cut out for selling. Against popular belief, good work doesn't always speak for itself; in films especially, a strong salesperson is needed to get projects seen and moving. Over time you will decide what kind of script editor you are, what your style is, and what your ultimate goals are, and you can arrange your efforts accordingly.

THE COMMON PURSUIT

The one thing everyone I interviewed had in common was a passionate desire to create outstanding material. Everyone agreed that finding a unique voice is the holy grail – a precious gift, made especially potent when the writer has a specific story to tell or is impassioned by something they wish to say. The most polished, best structured and slickest of scripts isn't necessarily the prized one, and won't automatically impress the reader. What proved far more important was the writer's voice, and the passion that came from their burning need to tell a particular story. I call this the heart of the writing, and it truly is what makes the strongest impact.

> *Screenwriting and development is about trial and error.*
> *For every good idea a writer has they will have a dozen*
> *weaker ideas, and for every good screenplay, there are a*
> *hundred times as many bad ones.*

That's not to say there aren't plenty of smart and extremely talented writers able to create all types of good work – it's just that there is something special that happens when all the elements align; when the appropriate writer for a project fully engages and connects to the subject matter, is supported and steered into doing their best work and does it wholeheartedly and completely. Those experiences are what we all aspire to and it is a mighty high target to achieve – but, oh, what a joy when you do.

If it were easy, or if that magic could be bottled and sold, there wouldn't be a need for the plethora of screenwriting books, courses and software, etc., available out there, and everyone would be doing it. But the truth is it's not easy; it's actually really hard, and all of us in the business of screenplay development are trying equally hard, with every project, to get it right. It's no wonder that there are tons of books and systems out there, all attempting to explain how to make the magic happen, because that is what we all want to achieve. And yes, there are tools that can really help along the way – but it does also take a bit of magic, or luck if you prefer to call it that, and that is out of our control. All we can do is constantly offer up our best efforts, using whichever of the tools help get us there, and continue to nurture the stories that inspire us, or scare us, or make us laugh, or cry... or simply just entertain us.

We are all mining for treasure – the treasure that exists in the hearts, minds and spirits of our precious writers. Treat them well, encourage them, and help them to create magic.

HOW TO GET STARTED
AS A SCRIPT EDITOR

One of the best ways to start a career in development is as a script reader, writing reports on scripts for producers. At first you'll probably have to offer your services for free, but that will give you a chance to gain experience and make contacts in the business.

Knowing how to evaluate a script is only a small part of what a script editor does, but it is the first important step towards honing the skills needed for the job.

> *Script reading is about assessment –*
> *script editing is about development.*

Focusing initially only on reading and evaluating scripts will allow you the chance to develop a strong foundation instead of taking on too much, too soon. The first step is being able to identify a well-told story, about something worth telling.

When I started out, I took classes, did internships and worked with mentors. I was living in the United States then, and although there were some great facilities available to me, such as the American Film Institute, numerous film schools and short courses, etc., I also created my own opportunities by approaching people whose work I respected and offering my assistance (without pay), in exchange for the chance to learn from them. I did this in spurts as I also had to support myself, but I found that many times, by helping out, I was in the right place at the right time, which soon led to paid work. Not always, and I certainly didn't go into those situations expecting it, but

I did get lucky on numerous occasions. Each project gave me more experience and confidence, more contacts in the industry, and slowly opportunities began to come my way and my progress continued.

Interning is one of the best ways to become a script reader. Getting work experience at a production company or with a literary agent, and working through their slush pile (collection of submitted scripts), is really the best way to get started. The world of interning has changed since I started out, as there are now greater restrictions, but nevertheless there are still opportunities out there and with determination you will find them.

Getting that first job can be very difficult, especially if you aren't in a position to intern or read for free, so try to get another job within a production company or agency – and offer to read scripts on the side in order to gain some experience. Networking is important, so try to find ways to meet people in the industry. Don't limit your approach to big production companies; it's the smaller ones that often need the help. Also, approach film competitions, theatre companies – anything to get your foot in the door.

When you do get an opportunity, make sure that you follow through by doing an excellent job. Make sure you put as much thought, care and insight into the work as possible, and that it meets the required brief and deadline.

Take as many courses and read as many books on screenwriting and related topics as you can in order to improve your skills and gain knowledge. I have been working in the field for over 20 years, and I still read the new industry books and take classes regularly to stay up to date and sharpen my skills.

Attending events such as film screenings and festivals is always inspiring and will greatly enhance your understanding of the industry. Universities, including the National Film and Television School, offer short courses, as do the Literary Consultancy, Arvon Courses and Retreats, and Euroscript.

Social media networks such as Talent Circle, Meetup, Facebook and Twitter can be really helpful in finding groups to work with and places to study, as well as gaining mentors and meeting people in the industry.

IN CONCLUSION

Screenwriting is a challenging undertaking and sometimes, when our focus is on supporting others, we actually forget just how hard what THEY are doing really is.

If you are in doubt, try writing a screenplay yourself.

I strongly believe that anyone whose job it is to support, review or comment on writers' work (or any artistic endeavour) should at some point experience what it is like to be the one under creative scrutiny. This is important, for the sake of having an understanding, respect and empathy with regard to the demands and stresses of the work. If you haven't been in that position, it's hard to imagine how exposed and disheartening the other side of the development process can feel, and how deeply comments and criticisms can sting. Believe me, having personal, first-hand experience will inform how you treat writers and give you an intimate understanding of the challenges they face.

The writer's best interests must take precedence and remain the priority at the heart of the development process.

Storytelling is such an individual, delicate, personal and subjective experience. Who has the right to say what is good or bad, right or wrong?

Well, in fact everyone… because whoever sees, reads or hears the story you're working on will have an experience AND an opinion.

One of the great joys of film is that we all get to have our own personal reaction. Each one of us has the right to say how we feel about a story, what we enjoyed, what we related to, what we learned, what we hoped for, and so on…

A writer's responsibility is to the material.

A script editor's responsibility is to respect that material, respect the writer, and respect the writer's work, while also guiding them towards an accomplished, succinct and filmable script. What I have hoped to do with this book is guide you in the same way, showing you the thought processes and underlying notions that script editors use to guide writers to their best work, so that their scripts are not only filmable, but exceptional.

SUGGESTED READING

In no particular order...

Reading Screenplays: How to Analyse and Evaluate Film Scripts by Lucy Scher

Into the Woods by John Yorke

Making a Good Script Great by Linda Seger

Screenwriting Updated: New (and Conventional) Ways of Writing for the Screen by Linda Aronson

The Anatomy of Story by John Truby

The Writer's Journey: Mythic Structure for Writers by Christopher Vogler

Writing for Television Series, Serials and Soaps by Yvonne Grace

The Coffee Break Screenwriter: Writing Your Script Ten Minutes at a Time by Pilar Alessandra

Essentials of Screenwriting by Richard Walter

Escaping into the Open: The art of writing true by Elizabeth Berg

Thinking in Pictures by John Sayles

The Art of Dramatic Writing by Lajos Egri

The Screenwriter's Workbook by Syd Field

Screenwriting 434 by Lew Hunter

Just Effing Entertain Me by Julie Gray

Save the Cat! by Blake Snyder

Adventures in the Screen Trade by William Goldman

Story: Substance, Structure, Style, and the Principles of Screenwriting by Robert McKee

Writing and Selling Drama Screenplays by Lucy V Hay

On Film-making by Alexander Mackendrick

Conversations with Wilder by Cameron Crowe
The Uses of Enchantment: the Meaning and Importance of Fairy Tales
   by Bruno Bettelheim
Poetics by Aristotle

USEFUL RESOURCES

http://karolgriffiths.com
for more information about me and my work
https://scriptangel.wordpress.com
Hayley McKenzie's blog is a great resource
www.johnaugust.com
a ton of useful information about screenwriting
www.bbc.co.uk/writersroom
www.afi.com (non-profit American Film Institute)
www.scriptadvice.co.uk
www.arvon.org
creative writing courses and retreats in the UK
www.scriptmag.com
www.londonscreenwritersfestival.com

FREE SCRIPT WEBSITES

www.simplyscripts.com
www.imsdb.com
www dailyscript.com
www.script-o-rama.com
www.mymoviescripts.com
www.joblo.com/moviescripts.php
www.bbc.co.uk/writersroom/scripts
www.thescriptlab.com

GLOSSARY OF FILM TERMS

A/B story: the 'A' story is the dramatic core of the movie. The primary storyline that main character follows. The 'B' story is a supporting storyline, or backstory, that runs parallel.

Above the line: is an industry term derived from where the money is budgeted for writers, directors, producers and principal talent. This term refers to job positions that are associated with the creative and/or financial control of a film, not the technical aspects. The distinction from 'below the line' originates from the early studio days when the budget top-sheet would literally have a line separating the above-the-line and below-the-line costs.

Act: sections that make up a unit of drama (also used to define structure).

Action block: a paragraph of descriptive script text. Action paragraphs describe the setting, physical actions, characters, and other important information.

Action: the scene description, character movement and elements as described in a screenplay.

Ad lib: improvised dialogue or action in spontaneous reaction to the given situation of a scene.

Adaptation: the process of rewriting/adapting fact or fiction from a written work into a movie, television drama or stage play.

Aerial shot: a shot taken from a plane or helicopter (not a crane).

Aftermath: a scene of aftermath follows a dramatically important scene and is used to give the characters and audience time to regroup from the shock, pain or joy of that moment. For example, bank robbers counting their haul after an intense heist.

Allegory: a symbolic work. An allegory is a story that sets out to reveal a moral lesson or hidden meaning. Films are generally not written as pure allegories with an objective of preaching, but fantasies and storybook films often have allegorical elements. (Allegorical characters also take on symbolic representations of moral meanings or lessons.)

Allusion: indirect but intentional references (or imitations) used to add greater depth or to link concepts to events and situations in a film. Associations are meant to indicate emotions, contrast and ironic twists. (A filmmaker's intentional reference to another film is called homage.)

Ambiguity: vagueness; a lack of transparency or an apparent contradiction in a storyline. Ambiguity can be used as an artistic tool to capture the imagination through confusion, as well as opposing perspectives and arguments. This is done intentionally in some films to stimulate thought, and unintentionally in others, as a result of weak writing. (Character ambiguity is used in the same way and can help progress or purposefully hinder the development of a character.)

Angle on: a shot description that informs the director that, although you are in the same location, the camera should now be pointed in a different direction. Usually occurs in scenes taking place in large settings. Should be used sparingly.

Angle: directs the camera in a particular way, for a particular shot of a person, location or object.

Antagonist: this character is the protagonist's main adversary. Not necessarily a villain, but has a single objective in conflict with the main character.

Anticlimax: a sudden decline in strength or importance. When there's a lot of build-up and the audience is expecting a peak in the action but it doesn't occur. Also anything that happens in the final few moments of a film that weakens the story conclusion and leaves the audience feeling let down and unsatisfied.

Anti-hero: a protagonist who has character defects or eccentricities, which are not usually associated with the hero archetype.

Archetypal characters: the term archetype refers to ancient patterns of personality that are the shared heritage of the human race. Similar to allegorical characters, their motifs are usually rooted in folklore; archetypal characters represent an ideal or symbolic image such as love, wisdom, heroism, villainy, forgiveness, etc.

Atmosphere: the mood, tone and impression of a film created by real or nebulous elements such as danger, severe weather or other suggestive components that add dimension to the setting. (Atmosphere is also a term used to refer to background actors.)

Audience awareness: a writer must determine whom they are writing their story for – and how they wish to involve their audience in the telling of it. Considerations include whether the audience should know story information before, after or at the same time as the characters involved, and how much mystery and suspense there should be. These decisions are part of crafting the script and writing with audience awareness.

b.g.: short for background and used to describe anything occurring in the background or rear plane of the foreground action. (Always written in lower-case initials.)

Back to scene: secondary heading that indicates the return to a scene after a montage or series of shots.

Background actor (also called an extra): a performer in a film or television show who appears in a non-speaking role, usually in the background. For example, in a busy street or crowd scene.

Backstory: historical background information that the writer creates for a character, contributing to their motivations and reactions, which either occurred in the past or is separate from the main plot. Backstory should not be telegraphed or forced, but should come out organically through conflict, humour and believable exposition.

Beat sheet: abbreviated description of the screenplay that details every scene of the story, and often indicates dialogue and character interactions. The scenes are often numbered for convenience. It can be an extremely useful tool for a writer. (Also called a step outline.)

beat: the parenthetical (beat) is used to interrupt a line of dialogue, telling an actor where to pause in a speech. (Always written in lower case.)

Below-the-line crew: refers to the technical crew hired for the length of the production; these individuals do not have primary creative or financial control of the project.

Below-the-line: is an industry term associated with the 'fixed' costs of a film. Examples include crew rates, studio fees, rental equipment and travel costs.

Block page: a script page that is dense with screen action description and very little white space. Visually, the page looks like a block of paragraphs. Screenwriters should try to avoid these kinds of pages as scripts need to move quickly; if possible they should break up description with a quick line of dialogue or by adding a new scene header and location.

Bookends: a structural technique in which a script begins and ends with a scene that encloses the whole and is used to show how characters have grown and changed.

Bridging shot: a shot used to cover a jump in time, place or other discontinuity, such as calendar pages flipping, an airplane flying, newspaper headlines or seasonal changes.

Build-up action (building a scene): the use of incidental shots and dramatic devices, such as increased tempo, volume and emphasis, to give greater meaning, clarity, suspense or excitement. Usually culminates with a major scene and is needed to complete coverage and visual storytelling to bring the scene to a climax.

Bump: a problematic element in a script that adversely deflects the reader's attention away from the story.

Button: mainly a comedy writing term referring to a witty line that ends or tops off a scene, but its meaning has expanded to include all genres and refers to the final line or incident that closes a scene.

Camera narrator: in film, the camera typically provides the point of view and the narration, showing the audience what is (or is not) happening.

Card: text printed on the screen that is needed to indicate information such as location, time, date or era.

Character: any person or individual appearing in a film.

Character arc: refers to the way the character changes and unfolds in their development, growth and transformation during the story (including how their point of view changes).

Character change: relates to the main character's arc. After going through the main tension and reaching the resolution, the character usually undergoes a significant change. That change is usually important and gratifying to an audience. However, on occasion, the point of a story is that a character change does not occur (or occur permanently). Used as a means to express a moral or convey a concept.

Character core: the character's core personality helps define who they are and should be interesting and flawed.

Character development: one of the major elements of screenwriting. Audiences look for characters who are relatable, diverse, interesting, sympathetic, and who seem well rounded and complete. To achieve this, the writer generates a background, creates a personality, physicality and psychology, along with flaws and goals.

Character emotions: a writer should develop all aspects of their characters, including concrete feelings and sentiments. Emotions deepen a character's humanity, even if the character doesn't entirely understand why or how they feel what they do. Having natural reactions makes the character more complete.

Character flaws: a weakness within the character that to a great extent defines them, such as jealousy, envy, selfishness, righteousness, paranoia, vengefulness, prejudice, etc. Character flaws will get the character into trouble and be used in their character arc in conjunction with lessons learned, typically changing by the end of the script.

Character identification: occurs when the audience feels connected to the character on an emotional level.

Character introduction (character description/character essence): when a new major or supporting character is introduced in a screenplay, writers should give a line or two of significant detail conveying the character, informing the reader of their essence and visual appearance (their age, look and noting anything special about them).

Character paradox: creating fascinating characters who surprise, challenge and change our preconceived notions about people is often accomplished through paradox. Paradox provides contradictory characteristics that make characters unique, unpredictable and memorable.

Character psychology: the writer must understand the psychology of their characters: what motivates them, why they behave in certain ways, and what their subconscious intentions are.

Character relationships: the chemistry between characters in a script is important to the overall story, and the screenwriter should use that chemistry to both bring characters together and create conflict between them.

Characterisation: describes traits and features in order to help portray a character, expressing the physical condition, mannerisms, language and style of speaking, style of dress, etc., of the characters.

Cheat a script: means to adjust the margins and spacing of a screenplay on the page (usually with a software program) in an attempt to make the script seem shorter than it really is.

Cliffhanger: an unresolved plot point that comes at the end of an act or story, created to increase interest for the next scene, episode or a sequel.

Climax: the highest point of tension in a film in which the central character faces, confronts and deals with the consequences of their decisions and actions, and/or faces the antagonist in a climactic battle or final engagement. Typically a crisis leads to the climax. Also called the film's high point/main culmination.

CLOSE ON: a shot description that suggests a close-up on some object, action or person. May also be seen as CLOSE-UP, C.U. or CLOSE SHOT.

Comic juxtaposition : the juxtaposition of two things that the audience doesn't expect to go together, but which have a point of reference that allows the writer to make a connection between them. What makes the juxtaposition funny is that it's not supposed to fit, but somehow it does.

Commentary: an objective opinion/description of characters/events occurring in the film, presented from an omniscient point of view by a commentator, presented as a voiceover. (Commentary also refers to one of the added features on DVDs in which the director, actors, producers or a film historian provide comments on the film in some way.)

Complication: a plot event that complicates or tightens the tension of a film.

Concept: the story idea or story premise; the central idea around which a screenplay is built.

Conflict: a struggle between two or more forces that creates a tension that must be resolved (although in some stories, as in real life, it isn't). The force that opposes a character and prevents them from achieving their goal. Conflict occurs when a character is in a difficult situation, facing obstacles, whether physical, social or psychological, that force them to take decisive action.

Context: the framework of what influences a character or a story, such as cultural elements, historical periods, locations, occupations, etc.

Continuing dialogue: dialogue spoken by the same character that continues uninterrupted onto the next page.

Continuity: the technical organisation of a film or television programme that makes it seem that the action happens without pauses or interruptions. Continuity also refers to the extent to which a film is consistent, without errors, jump cuts or mismatched shots or details. (A mistake or mismatch is called a continuity error.)

Continuous: a term used instead of DAY or NIGHT in a slug line, which indicates that the action moves from one location/scene to another without any interruptions in time.

Contrast: the marked difference between two characters, where they are distinguished by dissimilar or opposite qualities. Used especially in romantic comedies, buddy pictures and coming-of-age stories. Contrasting two characters who seemingly have nothing in common, but who, after further development, turn out to share common ground, is a strong way to achieve character dynamics.

Coverage: notes prepared for a literary agency or film production company giving a basic assessment of the script. Also refers to all the shots and angles that a director shoots of a scene. Having proper coverage means having a master shot and all the proper angles filmed of a scene (master shot, close-ups, reversals, etc.).

Crosscut (intercut): interweaving parts of two or more scenes in order to show simultaneous action.

Delay: a dramatic device used to increase tension by delaying the answer to a question, the arrival of an expected event or character, or the solution of a mystery in order to make a greater impact on an audience.

Denouement (resolution): the outcome or unravelling of the tension in the scenes after the climax of a film. How things turned out for all the characters.

Deus ex machina: usually refers to an unlikely, improbable, contrived, illogical or clumsy ending or suddenly appearing plot device that alleviates a difficult situation or brings about a resolution.

Diabolus ex machina: the introduction of an unexpected or arbitrary and unjustified obstacle designed to ensure that things suddenly get much worse for the protagonists.

Dialogue: any spoken lines in a film. Dialogue has multiple functions: to reveal characters, to move the plot forward, to guide the audience, and to deliver exposition and backstory.

Directing on the page: an expression used when a writer provides too many camera positions such as ZOOM IN, ANGLE ON, TRACKING SHOT, etc. When the writer does this they are potentially alienating the director, while also limiting what can be imagined of the script. The screenwriter should find ways of highlighting important objects/ beats without using camera shots.

Dissolve to: a transition between scenes in which two images gradually overlap each other.

Dramatic answer: the answer to the question posed in a drama. Can be positive, negative or unresolved (but this is rare and the ending still needs to be satisfying).

Dramatic conflict: obstacles in the story that make it difficult for the main character to achieve their goals.

Dramatic Irony: occurs when the audience gains information that at least one person on screen does not know. Because of this understanding, the words of the characters take on a different meaning. This can create intense suspense or humour. (For example, in *Star Wars*, the audience learns before Luke does that Darth Vader is his father, and this increases the tension.)

Dramatic need: unresolved issue facing the main character.

Dramatic question: centres on the protagonist's central conflict and asks: will the protagonist achieve their objective?

Dramatic structure: the characteristics needed for a drama. According to Aristotle, they are a beginning, middle and end. These elements include an explanation or revelation to the audience of what will be going on, a development in which the plot unfolds, a climax where all events come to a peak, and a conclusion when everything in the plot is unravelled and resolved.

Dramaturgy: the theory and practice of dramatic composition.

Dual dialogue: when two characters speak simultaneously, their dialogue is placed side by side on the script page.

Ellipsis: used to show dialogue trailing off, and when it continues again (...).

Empathy: the ability to understand and share the feelings of another. In a film it is considered important that the audience care about (or at least on some level relate to) the characters in the story – otherwise, they will not care about the character's objective. The writer can create empathy by placing the audience in a character's shoes and allowing both the character and the audience to discover what is at stake at the same time.

Environment: the surroundings and conditions in which a character lives and operates. (Environment can also be a source of conflict in a script, and sometimes is the antagonist of the story – a haunted house, stranded at sea, that sort of thing.)

Execution: the manner in which story elements are implemented, and their effectiveness.

Exposition: background information necessary to the understanding of the facts from which the story action departs, such as events occurring before the main plot, the setting, the characters, backstories, etc. Exposition can be conveyed through dialogue, flashbacks, dream sequences, characters' thoughts, background details or narration.

Extension: placed in parentheses to the right of the character name and denoting how the character's voice is heard, such as '(O.S.)', meaning off screen.

Exterior: listed at the beginning of the scene heading, informing the reader that the following scene will be outdoors. (Abbreviated as EXT. within the script.)

Fade in: a transitional shot. Historically, the first words typed in a script.

Fade out: when an image fades to black. Historically, the last words typed in a script.

Fade: gradual changes in the intensity of an image or sound to create a transition.

Falling action: the part of a script plot that occurs after the climax has been reached. It's the resolution of the obstacle that has been faced throughout. In some films there is no falling action, leaving the film open-ended for the audience to interpret as they like, or to set up a sequel. The span of time in the falling action is usually brief.

Fantasy characters: imaginary characters who live in a strange, romantic or magical setting. These characters are defined by their physical unusualness, or being 'super powered' in some way – super fast, super smart, etc.

First culmination (midpoint, mid-act climax or midpoint reversal): an important scene in the middle of the script, often a reversal of fortune or revelation that changes the direction of the story.

Flashback: a scene set in a time earlier than the main story of the film, taking the story to a previous or past event, scene or sequence. A flashback interrupts the action and is used to show the motivation, reaction, memory or dream of a character.

Flash-forward: the opposite of a flashback; a filmic technique that depicts a scene, event or sequence, imagined or expected, that is projected into a future time beyond the present time of the film.

Foreground: describes anything occurring in front of the main action. Usually abbreviated as 'f.g.'.

Foreshadowing: hints at story developments to come, in order to prepare the viewer for later events, revelations or plot resolutions. Uses symbolism, images, music, motifs, repetition, dialogue and mood to convey hints and build suspense.

Formula: refers to a method of structuring a script (meaning it must include certain elements and arrive at a certain ending).

Four-act structure: same as three-act structure, but the second act is divided into two acts at the midpoint.

Fourth wall: refers to the imaginary, illusory, invisible plane through which the film viewer or audience is thought to look at the action. The fourth wall separates the audience from the characters. It is 'broken' when the barrier between the fictional world of the film's story and the 'real world' of the audience is shattered; for example, when an actor speaks directly to viewers by making an aside (such as in *Ferris Bueller's Day Off*, *High Fidelity* and *Annie Hall*).

Freeze frame: an optical effect in which a single frame is identically repeated over several frames causing the action to stop and giving the illusion of a still photograph. Often used at the end of a film to indicate ambiguity, death or to provide a lasting image (such as *The Colour of Money*, *Staying Alive*, *Butch Cassidy and the Sundance Kid* and *An Officer and a Gentleman*).

FX or SPFX: the abbreviation for special or visual effects.

Genre conventions: standards used to plot character, setting, icon, theme or effect in a genre. (In Westerns, for example, it is a genre convention for the heroes to wear white hats, while the villains wear black ones.)

Genre hybridisation: a script that combines or intersects two or more distinct genre types, and cannot be categorised by a single genre (such as *Blade Runner*, which combines film noir with science fiction, or *Sweeney Todd*, which combines drama, horror and musical).

Genre iconography: recognised components that repeatedly tell the story. Stars can become icons for specific genres, such as Bruce Lee for martial arts films and John Wayne for Westerns.

Genre: categories used to describe screenplay conventions, which organise and group films according to repeated subjects, icons, styles and audience expectations.

Green-light: permission to proceed; to authorise a project. To green-light a project is to formally approve its production finance and to commit to this financing, thereby allowing the project to move forward from the development phase into pre-production and principal photography.

Header: the line printed at the top of a production script, which includes the date of the revision and the colour of the page. (A header occupies the same line as the page number, which is on the right, and is .5 from the top, for example, 'REVISED April 10, 2015 BLUE 1.')

Hero: refers to the protagonist (main character) in a script.

High concept: refers to a type of film that can be easily pitched or described, with a simple and succinct premise, for example: what if dinosaurs were cloned? What if a shark terrorised a beach town? A low concept story is more concerned with character development and other subtleties that aren't as easily summarised (*Sideways*, *Little Miss Sunshine*).

Hook: the concept or element that grabs the audience's attention; must be original and preferably introduced in the first five to ten minutes of the film. If the writer provides a strong hook, the reader/audience will probably want to see the story through till the end.

Inciting incident: the first major plot point. This moment usually occurs in the first ten pages of the script (but not always). This event disturbs the life of the protagonist and sets them off in pursuit of an objective. (The inciting incident is something that changes the main character's life so irrevocably that they can't ignore it; it's the event that kick-starts the core of story.)

Indirection: occurs when a character sees something he cannot hear – or hears something he cannot see – and acts based on this incomplete information.

Insert: this is used as a scene heading and describes a shot of some important detail, usually in reference to objects, such as a ticking clock, a gun, a poisoned drink, etc; something that must be given the camera's full attention. (It is followed by 'Back to scene' – or a new scene heading.) Alternatively, the object can be written in CAPS to convey its importance. Writers should use inserts sparingly.

Interior: listed at the beginning of the scene heading, informing the reader that the following scene will be indoors. (Abbreviated as INT. within the script.)

Interrupt: when a character cuts off another character's dialogue. This is either shown with an ellipsis (...) or an em dash (—).

Intrigue: keeping the audience interested. Showing the audience a character doing something that is not yet clear or understood will create intrigue, as will creating obstacles that make it difficult for the hero to achieve their goal.

Irony: device making a character use words, pursue actions or follow intentions that mean one thing to them, but something entirely different to the audience and the other characters.

Jump cut to: an abrupt transition in which two sequential shots of the same subject in the same scene in real time are taken from camera positions that vary only slightly. This type of edit causes the subject to appear to 'jump' position and gives the effect of jumping forwards in time.

Location: the properties or places (interior or exterior) in which a filmed scene takes place.

Locked: once the script is handed out to the talent and department heads in preparation for production, the pages must be LOCKED so that any changes made after this time are easily tracked. If any changes are made to the script after circulation, only the REVISED PAGES will be printed and distributed. The revised pages must be easily incorporated into the script without displacing or rearranging the original pages.

Lock-in: at the end of act one, the main character must be 'locked-in' to the predicament that is central to the story, propelling them in a new direction in order to obtain their goal.

Logline (or tagline): the story concept of a script/film in one short and snappy sentence conveying the central proposition of the film. Provides a tempting soundbite of the story and is used to sell tickets and printed on film posters.

Macguffin (or McGuffin): term created by Alfred Hitchcock for the plot device or element (an object, goal, event or piece of knowledge) that catches the viewer's attention or drives the logic or action of the plot and appears extremely important, but turns out to be less significant or often ignored after it has served its purpose (examples include the use of Rosebud in *Citizen Kane* and the priceless statue in *The Maltese Falcon*).

Main culmination (or climax): the highest point of anxiety or tension in a story or film in which the central character faces, confronts and deals with the consequences of all their actions, or faces the antagonist in a climactic battle or final engagement.

Master scene script: the format required by the motion picture industry for modern screenplays before they are green-lit for production. The master scene script is distinct from the shooting script in that it does not include camera direction or scene numbers.

Match cut to: a transitional technique; a cut in film editing between either two different objects, two different spaces or two different compositions in which objects in the two shots graphically match. A match cut often helps to establish a strong continuity of action by linking two shots metaphorically. (For example, in *2001: A Space Odyssey*, Stanley Kubrick uses a match cut after an ape discovers that bones can be used as tools and weapons. The ape triumphantly throws one into the air and, as it spins, there is a match cut to an orbiting nuclear weapons satellite. The match cut helps draw a connection between the two objects as weapons, and exemplifies humanity's technological advancement.)

Midpoint (mid-act climax or midpoint reversal): an important scene in the middle of the script, often a reversal of fortune or revelation that changes the direction of the story.

Midpoint contrast: rule of story structure. The first culmination/ midpoint and the main culmination (end of act two) should almost always contrast with each other. If one is tragic, the other should be happy and vice versa. (If the script has a tragic midpoint and end, then the protagonist should have a major victory at the end of act two.)

Monologue: a long speech by one character without interruption, usually lecturing to others and often when the conflict is at a high point.

Montage (or montage sequence): a series of shots or images showing a theme, an event, the passage of time, etc., all related and building to a conclusion.

Mood: the atmosphere or pervading tone.

MOS: term to describe a shot filmed without sound; originated with German director Erich von Stroheim.

Mystery: creates tension by presenting something unknown, puzzling or disturbing. It evokes the viewer's curiosity and asks them to solve the riddle.

Mythic characters: tend to be heroic characters who encourage and motivate us into new behaviours or understandings, aimed at making us better people. Usually moral lessons are connected with mythology, fables and folklore.

Non-linear: a screenplay in which events are ordered differently from their natural sequence in time.

Objective: a goal. The main character's objective is their want or need to accomplish something.

Obligatory scene: a scene that the viewer excitedly expects (usually relative to the genre), which creates anticipation, and typically expresses the theme of the film (for example, the first kiss in a romance).

Obstacles: the problems, hurdles, difficulties and conflicts that occur throughout the entire script and increase in difficulty as the story progresses (the building blocks of the second act). (External obstacle is not related to the character, but comes from outside. Internal obstacle is part of the character's nature.)

Off-camera (O.C.)/Off-screen (O.S.): often used interchangeably by writers, meaning they want the voice, action or sound in a scene to come from somewhere unseen. But these terms technically do have slightly different meanings. Traditionally, O.C. applies when a character does or says something whilst physically in the same space as the person listening/observing, but is just not on camera (i.e. not within the area being filmed). O.S. is used when the character speaking and the listener are in different places.

Opening credits: an introduction to the film that includes the title and selected important members of the production. Often superimposed on the action.

Opening: the first ten pages of a script. Typically, if a script has not made a favourable impression by this point, it will not be considered.

Opposition: resistance that usually comes from the antagonist.

Out of character: the description of a character who does or says something that is inconsistent with their established pattern of behaviour.

Overlapping dialogue: when two characters have simultaneous dialogue.

Parentheticals (wrylies): actor's instructions. Only to be used where a line of dialogue might be interpreted in some way contrary to logic.

Passive character: inactive character. A passive protagonist usually reacts to events rather than driving or affecting the story.

Payoff: the moment when something that was set up earlier becomes meaningful.

Pitch: a concise verbal and sometimes visual presentation of an idea for a film or television series. (Becomes visual by including storyboard art, research materials and images.)

Planting: a device by which a pattern such as a line of dialogue, or a gesture, or other element is introduced into a story and repeated. As the story progresses and the circumstances advance towards the resolution, the planted information assumes a new meaning and 'pays off'.

Plausibility: story believability, credibility, within the scope of the framework of the story.

Plot point: a key turning point or moment in a film's story that significantly advances the action or moves the story in a different direction.

Plot: the gist of a story. A series of dramatic events or actions that make up a film or story narrative. According to Aristotle, plot is the arrangement of a story's events such that one follows logically from the other.

THE ART OF SCRIPT EDITING

Point of attack: also called the inciting incident, this is the moment (the first major plot point) at which the dramatic conflict is announced. This moment usually occurs in the first ten pages of the script (but not always). This event disturbs the life of the protagonist and sets them off in pursuit of an objective.

Point of no return moment: usually in the first half of script, when the protagonist can't turn back from their journey and life will never be the same for them.

Point of view (POV): the perspective from which the film story is told. Also refers to a shot that depicts the outlook or position of a character.

Polarity: most dramatic stories contain polarity, which is the reversal from one experience to its opposite. For example, naiveté to maturity, rags to riches, hate to love.

Predictability: obviousness or unoriginality.

Premise line: a succinct description that conveys the meaning and essence of the script.

Props: objects used by characters in a scene. Not furniture or costumes, but portable items.

Protagonist: the protagonist is the leading character in the script. Serves as the focus of the plot, driving the story forward with their intentions and actions.

Raisonneur: a character (usually a supporting character) who helps the audience keep track of the values of the story and voices the central theme, philosophy or point of view of the work.

Ramifications: consequences.

Recognition: occurs when a character finds out what we (the audience) already know.

Red herring: a subplot or suggestion intended to mislead the audience.

Redundancies: unnecessary repetitious words or phrases in a screenplay.

Resolution (also known as the denouement): the outcome or unravelling of the tension in the scenes after the climax of a film. How things turned out for all the characters.

Reversal (or twist): a reversal is a surprising but explainable and motivated change in the direction of the action in a film. Can be within a scene, a sequence, or in the overall storyline.

Reverse angle: when the camera turns 180 degrees to get a shot from the polar opposite side. Often used to reveal things for comic or dramatic effect.

Rhythm: an essential feature of a film, for it decisively contributes to its mood and overall impression on the audience. Rhythm gets expressed not only by the actions of the characters and dialogue, but also in the editing of the shots, the sequences, and the sound and music used.

Rising action: the series of events that begin immediately after the introduction of the story and build up to the climax.

Rough cut: an early edited version of a film with all the pieces assembled in sequential order, but without any elaborate editing (also known as a first cut).

Running time: the length of a film or television show (how long the film runs in minutes).

Rushes (also known as dailies): the printed takes of the camera footage from one day's shooting. Usually viewed by the director and director of photography without correction or editing, before the next day's shooting.

Scenarios: the possible situations and plot outlines in a screenplay.

Scene cards: a method used by some writers to outline their script. Each scene gets outlined on an index card; the writer can then rearrange the order of the cards to work out the story structure.

Scene description: action that pushes the story forward and/or reveals character in as few words as possible (not just verbal description, but action that provides description).

Scene headings: occur at the start of every scene, stating whether the scene is interior (INT.) or exterior (EXT.), and list the specific location and time of day. For example: INT. JOHNNY'S APARTMENT – BEDROOM – NIGHT.

Scene: unit of action in the story containing its own beginning, middle and end as well as its own objective, character and conflict. Scenes can range from one shot to infinity and are distinguished by slug lines. The end of a scene is often indicated by a change in time, action and/or location.

Scenes of preparation: usually scenes of a character getting ready for the dramatic confrontation ahead. They are used to rev up the audience emotionally and prepare them for what comes later.

Screen direction: the direction that actors or objects appear to be moving on the screen from the point of view of the camera or audience. A rule of film editing is that movement from one edited shot to another must maintain the consistency of screen direction in order to avoid visual confusion for the audience. 'Camera left' or 'frame left' indicates movement towards the left side of the screen, while 'camera right' or 'frame right' refers to movement towards the right side of the screen. 'Foreground' refers to the space close to the camera (close to the audience), while 'background' refers to the space in the distance away from the camera and the audience.

Sequel (follow-up): a cinematic work that picks up the characters, settings and events of a story in a previously made or preceding movie.

Sequence: a series of scenes building a distinct narrative unit, usually connected either by unity of time, location or an event. It is a self-contained portion of the entire story (a group of scenes that follow one objective, such as a car-chase sequence).

Serial: a television (or radio) programme that relies on a continuing plot.

Series of shots: quick shots that tell a story.

Set-piece: a term used to describe any important dramatic or comedic highpoint in a film or story, particularly those that provide some kind of dramatic payoff, resolution or transition.

Setting: the time and place in which the story takes place.

Set-up: the process of laying the groundwork for a dramatic or comic situation that will later be resolved or paid off. Also refers to the function of the first act in introducing the story, and the problem that the story will try to resolve.

SFX: indicates sound effects.

Slug line: an upper-case line of text with a blank line above and below it. Often used interchangeably with scene heading, BUT more often refers to an intermediary slug line, which is used to break up a longer scene, or to refocus and point out an important detail or new element.

Smash cut: a stylistic and especially abrupt transition, often used to convey quick emotional changes, violence or destruction.

Soap opera: a serial drama on television (or radio) which features related storylines about the lives of multiple characters. The stories usually focus on emotional relationships to the point of melodrama.

Split screen: different scenes taking place in two or more sections of the screen. The scenes are usually interactive, such as showing two people in a phone conversation. However, split screen can also be used for separate events or flashbacks occurring simultaneously.

Stakes: what the character is risking; their reason for needing to obtain their objective. The stakes must be clear in order to show the audience how and why the tension is important, and what will happen if the character does not resolve their problem. Stakes should be high to warrant audience interest; often in films the stakes are a matter of life and death.

Status quo: the existing state of affairs for the main character.

Steadicam shot: a hand-held camera technique using a mechanical harness that allows the camera operator to take relatively smooth and steady hand-held shots, while moving along with the action. The resulting images are comparable to normal tracking shots on a wheeled dolly or can be made rougher to provide energy and movement to the action.

Step outline: a story outline of the major scenes, each described in just a few lines.

Stereotypical character: an oversimplified image or idea of a particular type of person. Screenwriters should avoid writing stereotypical characters unless they are deliberately designed for a specific reason.

Stock footage: footage of a location or event from other films and/or television broadcasts. They can be modern or historical and are used to save the company from having to shoot new (and often expensive) footage. (Example: *Friends* and *Seinfeld* were both shot in Los Angeles, but were meant to take place in New York. Stock footage/ shots were used in each episode to depict Manhattan.)

Story beats: the main points, twists and turns in the story.

Storyboards: illustrations or images that are organised and displayed in a sequence for the purpose of preparing and visualising the film. Often contain captions or shot/action descriptions.

Structure: the way in which events are organised in a script.

Style: a distinctive manner and means of expression used for a specific purpose.

Subplot (B story): a supporting storyline or backstory that runs parallel with the main story and has its own objective.

Subplot characters: used to initiate, help, complicate or hinder the hero's efforts. Can be connected with the main conflict, or used to either foil or support the conflict.

Subtext: what a character is saying between the lines, revealed by their actions and reactions.

Subtitles: superimposed words on the screen, which mirror the dialogue. Usually used to translate language or for the hearing-impaired.

Superimpose: the laying of one image over another and used in the same shot.

Supporting characters: used to interact in the story in ways that will affect and help us better understand the main character. Although they are 'supporting', they are vitally important and should be well rounded and layered. (An example of a strong supporting character is Darth Vader in the original *Star Wars* films.)

Suspense: a feeling of pleasurable fascination and excitement mixed with apprehension, enjoyable tension and anxiety, developed from the unpredictable, mysterious and rousing content of a film.

Symbolic characters: one-dimensional characters often found in non-realistic worlds such as fantasy, sci-fi, superhero and comic-book stories. They usually personify a quality or idea, such as love, innocence, wisdom, or justice.

Sympathy: occurs when the audience has feelings of empathy or pity for a character's misfortune. Sympathetic characters help to engage an audience's participation with the story.

Synopsis: a summary of the screenplay told in the present tense (ideally only three paragraphs long).

Tag: a short scene at the end of a movie or TV show that ties up loose ends or provides an upbeat addition to the climax.

Tagline (logline): the story concept of a script/film in one short and snappy sentence conveying the central proposition of the film. Provides a tempting soundbite of the story and is used to sell tickets and printed on film posters.

Teaser: brief initial scene that establishes a TV show episode.

Telegraph: making something overly obvious to the audience or setting it up clumsily.

Tension: feeling of fear and excitement created and built up by the writer of a film, consisting of hope for a desired outcome and, simultaneously, fear that the opposite will happen.

Thematic conflict: what ideas, truths or life issues are being explored in the story? Consider the thematic quality that seems prevalent in a script and then determine its opposite. So, if greed is the main theme, generosity is the opposite – using those two themes in the story creates thematic conflict. (Include both in your premise – 'Greed versus Generosity'.)

Theme: the moral message that the writer weaves intentionally throughout the story; the overriding idea behind the story, and the meaning of the experience that has just been presented.

Three-act structure: the classical form of storytelling based on Aristotle's dramatic structure, which includes the set-up, the complication and the resolution (beginning, middle and end).

Ticking clock: a dramatic device that increases the tension, in which some event looming in the near future requires that the conflict reach a speedy resolution.

Tone: the prevailing character and colour of the writing. The way it feels and sounds.

Transition shot: a shot designed to move one scene to another.

Treatment: a scene-by-scene description of a screenplay, told in present tense and generally with no dialogue. Length varies, but typically runs 20 pages.

Twist (or reversal): a plot point that is a major surprise to the audience, yet is an explainable and motivated change in the direction of the action, either within a scene, a sequence, or in the overall storyline.

Unity: refers to a script's cohesiveness. In a unified script, all the elements work subtly together to create a congruous whole.

Vertical reading: scripts that have a lot of white space, which helps the reader to skim quickly, shot by shot, and see the film as the writer envisioned it.

Visuals: show – don't tell. The writer must avoid explaining too much to the audience and should reveal information bit by bit, encouraging the audience to actively experience the story unfolding. A script should ignite the reader's imagination, from start to finish.

Voice: the embodied expression. How and what a writer or character has to say. A unique, distinct and entertaining voice is the holy grail of script development!

Voiceover (V.O.): dialogue by a character not in the scene, or not seen speaking the dialogue. Used to indicate a character is speaking via telephone, or for narration.

White space: the unwritten-on portions of a script page. White space helps the reader move quickly through the pages; the more white space the page has, the more vertical the script becomes, making it a faster read. Having white space gives the script a clean, uncluttered aesthetic that assures the reader that the story is told with confidence, focus and precision.

Word play (wordplay): is a literary technique and form of verbal wit based on the meanings and ambiguities of words, puns and clever repartee in which the words that are used become the main subject of the work, primarily for the purpose of intended effect or amusement.

World of the story: the world in which the story unfolds. Whatever story a writer is telling, they must also create the world that supports it. The writer must be specific, taking the audience to a well-defined and exact place (real or imaginary).